Comparing

185 396 3577

Comparing Nurseries

Staff and children in Italy, Spain and the UK

Helen Penn

P·C·P

**Paul Chapman
Publishing Ltd**

Paul Chapman Publishing Ltd
A SAGE Publications Company
6 Bonhill Street
London EC2A 4PU

British Library Cataloguing in Publication Data
Penn, Helen
Comparing nurseries: staff and children in Italy, Spain and the UK
1. Education, Preschool – Europe – Cross-cultural studies
I. Title
372.2'1'094

ISBN 1 85396 357 7

Typeset by Anneset, Weston Super Mare, Somerset
Printed and bound in Great Britain by
Athenæum Press Ltd, Gateshead, Tyne & Wear

C D E F G H 3 2 1 0 9

Contents

Foreword

Recent years have seen an explosion of crossnational studies comparing early childhood services in different countries. Most of these studies have been at a very general level, comparing policies, levels of provision, standards, systems and so on in different countries. This book, by contrast, takes us to another level – into the nursery. Helen Penn presents unique and rich material about the philosophy, culture, organization and practice in 12 nurseries in three countries, providing a perfect complement to the macrolevel work.

Case studies always raise questions about generalizability. The nurseries studied in Italy and Spain are located in areas – the region of Emilia-Romagna and the city of Barcelona – which are recognized as having particularly high standards in their services and which are among the most socially and economically advanced areas in their respective countries. The English nurseries are located in a particularly disadvantaged area of England; the picture presented of poverty and devastated communities is shocking. Being council run, these day nurseries are now in a minority of day nursery provision and have the particularly challenging (some might say impossible) role of working predominantly with children from highly distressed and vulnerable families. In the segregated market-oriented services of contemporary England, most day nurseries are now run privately, providing care for children whose working parents can afford to buy the service.

Yet despite these qualifications, there are a number of revealing differences between the nurseries in the three countries which can be said to apply more generally. In the UK, early childhood services are split between education and welfare, the former responsible for 'nursery schooling', the latter for 'childcare for working parents' and (what the English nurseries offered) 'daycare for children in need'. In contrast, the nurseries in Italy and Spain operated in settings which challenged this split between care and education. While the national government in Italy continues to divide responsibility for early childhood services between Ministries for Health and Education, most nurseries in Italy are the responsibility of local authority education departments and are treated, locally, as part of the education system. In Spain, major education reform legislation in 1990 made 0–6 years the first stage of the education system, and made the education system responsible for all services for this age group; in effect a national framework has been put in place for the development of an integrated early childhood service, although much remains to be done before that ideal becomes a reality. In short, while the UK still compartmentalizes services, Italy and Spain have moved a long way down the road to recognizing that care and education are inseparable.

This structural difference is matched by a strong ideological difference about the role of government. The four English nurseries operate in a policy regime which has long asserted that public responsibility for 'daycare' (itself a term born and bred of a divided approach to early childhood services) is limited to a small minority of children defined by social work agencies as being 'in need'. The flavour is caught in this recent ministerial pronouncement: 'I do not believe in the "nanny state". It is not Government's job to look after children – except of course where there is real need. That is properly parents' responsibility' (Foreword by Ms Cheryl Gillan, MP, to DfEE, 1996). By contrast, the nurseries in Italy and Spain operate in a political climate which recognizes a much wider public responsibility towards the provision of services for young children, including children with working parents – treating children as a shared responsibility between parents and society, rather than as a private concern of parents.

Moving into the nurseries, these cases illustrate different attitudes to staffing in England on the one hand and Italy and Spain on the other. There is a much higher commitment to staff training in Spain and Italy. In Spain, basic training has been revolutionized by the introduction of a new three-year, post-18 qualification, as an early childhood teacher, covering children from 0 to 6; 80% of staff in the Barcelona nurseries have this qualification. Basic training in Italy remains weak, but is supplemented by a powerful commitment to continuous training, enabled by giving each staff member six hours of non-contact time per week and providing pedagogical co-ordinators to help with the development of training programmes. Despite the stronger basic training in Spain, the Barcelona nurseries also emphasize the need for continuous training. This training is essential to the whole orientation of the nurseries. As Helen points out: 'in Italy and Spain a great deal of emphasis was put on how the nursery as a whole could review and develop its practice and think critically about it. Review and development were integral to the service.' By contrast, the staff in English nurseries have, generally, poor levels of basic training (the NNEB qualification) and little continuous training – and no ethos of critical review and development. What the English nurseries do offer was higher staffing levels, levels so high in fact that Helen suggest that there was often overstaffing. These levels conform to the standards laid down in the Children Act guidelines.

Comparison between the three countries illustrate that staffing ratios by themselves are of limited relevance. High staffing levels alone do not ensure or even increase the likelihood of good work. Far more important is to take a global view of staffing, covering a range of issues including basic and continuous training, and based on a concept or vision of what nurseries are for and about – a point to which I shall return.

Another of these staffing issues is highlighted by the case studies – management and organization. All 12 nurseries were publicly funded and the responsibility of local authorities. But whereas the Italian and Spanish nurseries were run on co-operative lines, with minimal hierarchies, the English nurseries were very hierarchical. While recognizing that these differences reflect strong historical and political differences – successful co-operatives cannot simply be willed – Helen's critique of the 'leadership' model in nurseries raises important questions.

The staffing structure in the English nurseries encourages the staff to see themselves as individuals rather than, as in Italy and Spain, as part of a group: 'in the English nurseries, by comparison with the collective nurseries of Italy and Spain, there was little sense of a committed group of staff sharing and working towards common objectives.' This individual–group difference also figures strongly in the approach taken to working with children. In an important section of the book, Helen highlights how the English nurseries differed from the Italian and Spanish nurseries:

> This fragmented and individualistic approach [in the English nurseries] was mirrored with the children . . . There was little sense of the children as a group able to influence or to help each other, and in general the organizational format of the nurseries would make it difficult to achieve, even if it were considered a worthwhile objective. The overall objective was instead the surveillance and monitoring of individual children to make sure they did not come to harm . . . in so far as any theoretical assumptions underpinned the approach to children in the UK nurseries, it was that of Bowlby

... [which] holds that emotional security, and therefore learning, only takes place in a one-to-one adult–child relationship, and all other situations are irrelevant. The contribution of the peer group is completely disregarded.

In contrast, and influenced by the work of the Italian educational theorist, Loris Malaguzzi, the peer group and the relationships between children were the key concept for the Italian and Spanish nurseries, the basis for understanding how young children learn and develop.

This individualistic approach in the English nurseries is a product of what Helen refers to as a 'poverty of theory':

[The staff] had no articulated rationale for their practices, only half-remembered and ill-digested ideas about child development and learning and attachment theory ... I would argue that this is mainly because there was no theory of pedagogy on which to draw. What should children be doing in nurseries? How is that different from the way they learn and behave at home? ... Not only was there no critical idea of what or how children might learn in the day nurseries or what kind of repertoire of activities might be available to them but there was also no idea about how children might behave together.

In a particularly challenging part of the book, Helen argues the 'irrelevance of theory in child development as a guide to practice' and draws attention to the increasing criticism of traditional child development, both from outside and within the profession. The Italian and Spanish nurseries have managed to develop a distinctive nursery pedagogy by drawing on a far wider range of theories and escaping some of this Anglo-American preoccupation with individuality. (One implicit lesson of the book is the need to value and protect diversity in the philosophy, organization and practice of early childhood services in the face of the growing influence of American developmental psychology research and neoliberal policy prescriptions.)

This individualistic approach to staff and children in the English nurseries is, I would suggest, part and parcel of an individualistic concept of early childhood services that has taken strong root in the Anglo-American approach to early childhood services. In the case of the council day nurseries, they are conceived of as a means to deliver a programme or intervention to individual children and families – in the same way as nursery schooling delivers educational interventions to a wider cross-section of children (what might be called the service-as-hyperdermic-syringe model). In the larger 'daycare' field, private nurseries and other services are conceptualized as selling a product ('childcare') to an individual consumer (the parent or the employer, depending on who foots the bill). What is missing is any sense of services as institutions of social and cultural significance to local communities and society at large.

The social significance of early childhood institutions can be seen in a number of ways. Nurseries can contribute to social cohesion and integration or to social atomization and exclusion. They can be a social resource for their local community, responsive to that community's needs, or a commodity to be purchased. They can foster social relationships based on reciprocity and co-operation or emphasize individual activities and development. They can signify that young children are citizens, with a recognized place in society as well as the family, with a voice to be listened to and the ability to participate actively; or they can signify that children are the dependent property of their parents, with no place outside the family unless the family fails in some major respect.

On these parameters of social significance, the Italian and Spanish nurseries are at the opposite ends to the English nurseries. There are similar differences when we consider cultural significance, and these are well illustrated throughout the book. Let me give just four examples.

First, the emphasis on relationships and activities between children makes it clear that the Spanish and Italian nurseries are places that foster a children's culture, providing space and opportunities for children to explore and produce their own means of expression. Second, nurseries are places where values and beliefs are transmitted. For example, in most of the Spanish and Italian nurseries, there is a strong emphasis on democracy, autonomy and egalitarianism. In the nurseries in all three counties, the almost totally female workforce transmits an ideology that working with children is women's work, a reminder that the cultural role of nurseries needs not only to be recognized but also reflected upon. Third, the nurseries in Barcelona had a very important role in sustaining the local Catalan culture through, for example, language (the children speak Catalan rather than Castilian in the nurseries) and food (which is given high priority in both the Spanish and Italian nurseries). Finally, nurseries can also be places that introduce young children to aesthetic culture – painting, sculpture, music and so on. One of the most striking images in the book is the children in the Barcelona nurseries engaging with Miro (the Catalan artist) and Mozart. Of course, Miro and Mozart represent only one strand of cultural activity, and there are many other cultures to whose influence children can be exposed – but nurseries can be places that expand children's horizons, rather than restrict them to the banalities of Walt Disney wall coverings and commercialized nursery rhymes.

The sad thing is that the idea that nurseries are institutions of social and cultural significance, not just businesses or service delivery systems, never figures in public policy in the UK. Helen rightly concludes that something is badly wrong in the UK, which is not a failure of the individuals working in nurseries and other services but 'a failure of the system at every level, from the theoretical to the political to the practical'. Over the years, we have managed to develop a system of early childhood services that is incoherent, inflexible, wasteful of resources, segregated and exclusive; finishes too soon, with the admission of most children at 4 into primary school (in contrast to the age of 6 in Italy, Spain and most other European countries); and is kept going by a large, dedicated and exploited workforce of poorly trained, poorly paid and poorly treated women.

In a centralized country like the UK (Italy and Spain have been decentralizing power in recent years, while power has been increasingly concentrated in the UK), a heavy responsibility must lie with central government for failing to provide vision and direction. The state we are in in the UK is the result of years of neglect by successive governments, in which ageing policies have been subject neither to reflection nor review, interspersed by occasional initiatives which fail to address the problems in early childhood, services and often make them worse by taking a narrow and sectional perspective – the Children Act, nursery vouchers and the recent government consultative paper on childcare options are but three of the most recent examples, where a blinkered approach has enabled one part of early childhood services to be considered in isolation from other parts. The frustration and inspiration of this book is that it shows us what nurseries, viewed seriously as social and cultural institutions, could offer to the lives of our children, families and communities, places like the wonderful nursery in Barcelona and conviviality and *joie de vivre*, of love and friendship, of affection and caring, of fun and laughter, of good food and good art, of creativity and learning.

Peter Moss

Acknowledgements

I am very grateful to all those who helped in the research and in the preparation of this book: Emmanuela Cocever, Raffaella Bassi, Irene Balaguer, Pepa Odena, Jane Streather and Susan McQuail. I am very glad they have all remained friends despite what I have to say. Last but not least I would like to thank all those who welcomed me into their nurseries and who were so patient in dealing with my inquiries. I also offer a special thank you to the cooks in the nurseries, whose contribution is so often under-rated.

1

Introduction

---

*What is the most difficult of all? That which seems to you the easiest, to
see with one's eyes what is lying before them*

(Goethe)

This book is about 12 nurseries, how they are organized, who
works in them and which children attend them. In particular it
explores what staff think about the work they are doing, how they
view and categorize it, and whether or not they like and enjoy it.
It traces how those views and opinions are translated into action
and how they impact on the children. Four of these nurseries are
in Italy, four in Spain and four in the UK, and the book also
explores what contribution the context and location of the nurseries makes to their practice.

A comparative study

I set about this study with some trepidation. I had been commissioned by the European Childcare Network to co-author a discussion document on the meaning of quality in early years
provision (Balaguer *et al.*, 1992). As part of this work I visited nurseries and talked to administrators in a number of European countries. This information was tantalizing and the diversity of what
I had seen made me think about and view nursery practices in
the UK in a different light. I decided I would like to find out more,
in as systematic a way possible, about how these different nurseries worked, although I knew that setting up and managing such
a systematic study across several countries would be very difficult.

I chose to work in Italy and Spain partly because, for reasons
described later, they are both countries with interesting and considered philosophies about childcare and education and in that
sense offered a useful contrast to the Anglo-American frame of

reference which dominates work in the UK. But I also made my choices for pragmatic reasons. The local authorities and local institutions I approached were willing to fund the study – no small consideration!

Quite apart from raising the funding to undertake an investigation, comparative studies are notoriously tricky. It is impossible to compare like with like because the contexts vary so much and what works well in one country or region may be an inappropriate solution in another. In particular concepts about early childhood do not translate easily. For instance words like 'childminder' or 'family daycarer' or 'playgroup' which carry a history and legitimacy in an English context are very difficult to describe in Spanish or Italian; conversely the concepts of *asilo nido* or *guarderia* which describe nurseries for children under 3 have no meaning or context in the UK. There is no direct equivalence in the type or availability of services from one country to another.

Not surprisingly – given the range and diversity of services – neither are there directly comparable statistics across the three countries described here. Even within the UK, the available statistics on types of service and take-up of services are themselves confused and contradictory and there is no common system of data collection between the different UK government departments responsible for early childhood services (Bull *et al.*, 1994). The European Childcare Network has made a rigorous attempt to document and compare services across member states, and Table 1.1 gives some useful indication of the figures available; but although they may provide rough grounds for comparison, such bald data cannot illuminate the differences; they have to be supplemented by a qualitative picture which paints more vividly what is going on.

To compound matters the system of local government is different in each country. Spain and Italy have a three-tier system: the commune or district, the region and the state. The communes and the regions have considerable autonomy in setting policy and raising revenue, and in the areas where I was carrying out the research these powers had been used fully to the benefit of early childhood services. In the UK, for education and social services there is only a two-tier system, the state and the local authority; and for the last 20 years, the powers of the local authority have been diminished and they have relatively few powers either for setting policy or for raising revenue. I have tried to give an account of these systems, and the kinds of

Table 1.1 Provision of publicly funded services in member states

| | A | B | C | D | Provision of publicly funded services for children (years) | | |
					0–3	3–6	6–10
Belgium	27	**	6	93	30%	95%+	??
Denmark	30	**	7	94	48%	82%	62% + all 6-year-olds in preprimary education
Germany	36	*	6	90	2% (W) 50% (E)	78% (W) 100% (E)	5% (W) 88% (E)
Greece	9	**	6	93	#3%	#70%(a)	?< 5%
Spain	36	*	6	93	?2%	84%	??
France	36	**	6	93	23%	99%	?30%
Ireland	3		6	93	2%	55%	?< 5%
Italy	9		6	91	6%	91%	??
The Netherlands	15	**	5	93	#8% (a)	#71% (a)	?< 5%
Austria	24		6	94	3%	75%	6%
Portugal	27		6	93	12%	48%	10%
Finland	36		7	94	21%	53%	5% + 60% of 6-year-olds in welfare and education system services
Sweden	36		7	94	33%	72%	64% + some 6-year-olds in preprimary schooling
UK	7	*	5	93	2%	#60% (a)	??< 5%

Notes

Column A gives the length of maternity leave + parental leave in months available per family after the birth of each child.

Column B indicates whether subsidies are available to parents (in addition to subsidies paid direct to services) to cover part of their costs for using services for young children.

* = subsidy available to lower-income parents only; ** = subsidy available to some/all parents, irrespective of income.

Source: European Commission Network on Childcare, 1996, p. 148.

services they have led to in the next chapter.

Add to all this difficulties with language and translation. The language itself is a major obstacle. One has to be a very fluent speaker to catch all the nuances and idioms of a language, and it is impossible to work with simultaneous or sequential translation in a project which relies solely on observation or interviews. So I had to devise a way of working which as far as possible took account of these difficulties of context, and reduced the costs and problems of translation. I explain very briefly at the beginning of each chapter how the work was undertaken.

Yet despite all these daunting obstacles it is enriching to explore how other people in other settings take on the task of working with young children; it enables you to reflect more deeply on everyday practices which are normally taken for granted. My experience working in early childhood services in the UK for many years both as an administrator and as a researcher is that whilst some of the practices I have observed have been enhancing for the children and adults who take part in them, many other practices are arbitrary and counterproductive. This point of view is elaborated in some length in *Transforming Nursery Education* (Moss and Penn, 1996). Here I try to show how well some of the children fare in their nurseries, and how much the staff enjoy their work with them; and conversely how unhappy children and staff can be in other situations. The comparative material brings all this into sharper focus and shows how exceptional and generous practices can be generated and, on the other hand, how ways of working regarded as normal and unchangeable are in fact abnormal and in urgent need of change.

The nature of practice and how it is influenced

For the staff who work in nurseries, their immediate situation and the daily practices with children which have been evolved within their nursery are what they think about first when asked to reflect on their practice. Like all professional practitioners the nursery workers organize their own work – within the limits set by their workplace – and take responsibility for their own effectiveness; how they relate to the children and what they provide for them is seen as a matter of professional skill and training. One worker I met vividly likened her own and her colleagues' work to those of artisans, proud of their craft working with children – although a craft-based model is in one sense a recipe for tradition and conservatism, a continuation and polishing of an accepted method rather than an openness to what is new.

In each country children and childhood have different meanings and status; and there are powerful historical, cultural and political traditions which permeate city, regional and national life. This is true for each of the localities where the nurseries are to be found. From the point of view of an outside observer such as myself looking at how much the 12 nurseries differed from one another, this wider sociocultural context was striking. It shaped and determined daily practice and set the parameters of what was possible, even though the practitioners themselves took their situation for granted.

The nature of children and the regard for childhood

What of the children themselves? One of my Italian translators, a charming young man, expressed considerable puzzlement when I tried to explain the project to him. 'But aren't all small children the same?' he said. His view, which is a common one amongst those who are unfamiliar with them, was that very young children were too young to be real people or to have individual wishes and needs, and therefore they did not require much more than physical care. On the contrary there is powerful evidence that very young children have overwhelming emotions, and since they are not yet articulate in expressing themselves they are dependent on adults for the way in which these feelings are understood and mediated (Goldschmied and Jackson, 1994). Young children are also vigorous learners keen to construct their own meanings, to interpret and make sense of what they see and do and feel.

In another way too the translator shared a common misperception. Childhood is a time of rich individuality but childhood itself is also a social and cultural construct (Brannen and O'Brien, 1995). Small children may follow similar stages and patterns of development, but it is fairly well established from crosscultural studies, particularly those involving Majority world children and families, that the specific skills children possess, and the expectations that are held of them by their families and other adults, are context specific. To take one example, the grace, physical agility, balance and stamina that are expected of very young children in some cultures are discouraged in others and seen as exposing children to physical danger and risk (Mead, 1963); or the way in which small children in many African cultures are routinely expect to take care of still younger children is often regarded as an unacceptable burden in western society; or the respect and deference for elders which young children are required to show in some Asian communities may be viewed as oppression in the west (Belle, 1989). A longitudinal study by Serpell (1993) in Zambia showed how the rural communities with whom he was working construed intelligence as inseparable from helpfulness – since the concept of intelligence essentially revolved around social alacrity and respect and understanding and willingness to meet the needs of others, an unhelpful child may be superficially 'school-clever' but could never be described as intelligent. These are perhaps extreme examples, but this same process of sociocultural diversity applies everywhere, and it is part of the claim of this book that it is a process which is often under-rated by many professionals who assume their own practices, beliefs and justifications to be universal. As the eminent psychologist William Kessen (1993, p. 228) writes: 'We have not faced the awesome variety of mankind. Rather our categories serve to limit the variety so that we can control it in our speaking and writing.'

Children then are representatives and products of the local communities and countries where they live. In the case of Italy, Spain and the UK there are substantial differences in how they live and in how resources and services for children are shared out. For instance, although in the study I was looking at publicly funded day nurseries which claimed to provide a service for those who needed it most, the interpretation of 'need' was very different in each community. The towns I visited in northern Italy, although run by communist-left parties, were some of the richest in Europe; distribution of wealth is relatively egalitarian, and cycling around the towns (as a remarkable cross-section of the public does, from elderly women in fur coats to young boys going to school) one sees few visible signs of poverty. The children who attended the Italian nurseries were well dressed and healthy and robust, and their parents seemed smart and prosperous. The UK nurseries, in a city of a similar size, were located in very poor and deprived areas, where there was a high level of vandalism and graffiti, with roaming dogs, burnt-out and boarded-up shops, broken glass and litter. One nursery required its own night-time security guard. The children in these nurseries looked woebegone and were often in poor health and many of the parents were down-at-heel and depressed men and women. The dispossession that seemed omnipresent in the UK city was hard to spot in the Italian city. I could have tried to find an English city in the more prosperous south east in a graffiti-free location but had I done so there almost certainly would have been no publicly funded day nurseries. In the UK the publicly funded day nurseries exist for the most deprived children. For the rest they are thought not to be necessary – nor perhaps to be appropriate. The day nurseries were an *expression* of inequalities between rich and poor in the UK, a level of inequality, which, as many commentators point out, is one of the distinguishing features of UK society (Hutton, 1995) just as in Italy they were an expression of the civic well-being (Putman, 1976; Malaguzzi 1993). The general conception of what a nursery is and does and whom it is for cannot but shape its practice – a theme I return to again and again.

The criteria for asking questions

I was interested in describing the daily practices in the nurseries I visited. For the reasons stated above, the cultural perceptions of children and childhood, and the social and economic circumstances of communities, this was not an easy topic of investigation. If I were to ask this question about schools, and ask what is an effective school, then the answer is easier. Schooling is a universal service, provided as of right to everybody. A good school is one which promotes learning; an effective school is one where the pupils achieve more academically than could be predicted from their intake. This definition is widely upheld across many countries and increasingly there are standard indicators which can be used to measure it (Salmon *et al.*, 1995). But there is less consensus about what nursery provision is for, and what aims it should have and how its achievements can be measured.

For some, what goes on in nurseries is merely a relaxed kind of schooling, and the same criteria of stimulating cognitive development and promoting learning are adopted, although the methods – it is hoped – differ from formal schooling. Children are assumed to play in order to learn, and it is perceived as the job of a skilled teacher to exploit the opportunities for playing and learning as fully as possible. For others, a nursery is a place where, whilst their mothers and fathers are at work, children may enjoy themselves and feel comfortable and secure and at ease; and the learning, although it is hoped takes place, is incidental. It is not necessarily regarded as the job of the staff to promote it. These two approaches are often characterized as an education versus a care approach.

In many countries the distinction between education and care is blurred but in the UK where schooling starts early there is a sharp dichotomy between care and education, and nursery education, as a matter of policy, excludes care (Moss and Penn, 1996) and even if its proponents wish otherwise, it cannot offer much in the way of care because its hours are so short – usually no more than two or two and a half hours per day in school settings during school terms. Moreover in the UK no publicly funded early childhood services are designed to care for working parents, and indeed one of the most recent of governmental consultation documents states firmly that the care of children is the responsibility of their parents, and by implication, no one else should be expected to carry the financial cost of that care (DfEE, 1996). As a result care for working parents is almost entirely provided within the private sector, available only to those who can afford to pay for it.

Other than education, as indicated above, the publicly funded care services which do exist are welfare based, and cater for 'children in need' usually defined as children from highly distressed and vulnerable families; and the aim of the service is to offer regular surveillance and protection for such children. (However the muddle in the UK is so great that each government department or sector can produce a document on early childhood without reference to any other sector, and the glaring inconsistencies between education, care and welfare approaches are blandly ignored. The recent education voucher scheme is an example of this disjointed thinking. At the same time as one section of the DfEE have introduced a scheme to give money directly to parents of 4-year-olds to buy nursery education, if necessary in day nurseries, another part of the DfEE continues to reiterate that the government has no obligation to pay towards parents' costs! Moreover the voucher scheme introduces a new system of inspection for the same nurseries which are already being inspected under welfare regulations introduced under the Children Act 1989. One hopes that such incoherence will sink under its own contradictions, and soon become history.)

The UK represents one extreme in providing for young children in assuming different kinds of services are necessary for different groups of children. At the other extreme – and both Spain and Italy lie near this end of the continuum – it is envisaged that one type of service can cater for all these needs, and provide education, care for children of working parents and protection for vulnerable children so that nurseries can be 'multifunctional'.

As well as care orientations and educational philosophies, there are many values which inform nurseries, and in one sense nurseries can only be judged as good or bad in terms of what the providers set out to offer (Petrie, 1994). These questions about aims and values recur continually throughout the book.

For instance one significant value held by the Spanish and Italian nurseries was an unshakeable belief in egalitarianism. In those countries I visited the nurseries were run as collectives, without managers or hierarchies and with no differences in gradings and no prospects of promotion. No one was in charge, and decisions were taken collectively. In the UK this type of organization carries the connotation of 1960s' style 'hippy communes' or worse still, anarchy, and there are few if any collective traditions of working in any sphere of activity. On the contrary notions of leadership and management are so embedded even in nurseries that it is hard to conceive of any organization functioning effectively without such a hierarchical basis. Yet the principle on which the Spanish and Italian nurseries were organized was that in a co-operative and collectively organized nursery the adults will have more egalitarian relationships with each other and with the children, and the children will in turn model their relationships with each other on this co-operative and collective pattern.

As the crosscultural studies have indicated, one of the key dimensions along which child-rearing differs is that of individualism versus collectivism. As Lamb *et al.* (1992, p. 11) comment, 'In the USA some view assertiveness as a desirable characteristic, whereas others view it as one manifestation of undesirable aggression. Everywhere debate persists over the relative value of individualism and co-operation'. This was clearly an important issue for this study, since the implicit rationale for collective working was that it made a difference to the co-operativeness of the children. So I was concerned to see how practices of staff reflected this belief in egalitarianism and to note how the children were encouraged to work and play together in each of the nurseries.

What theorists say

It is clear then that no simple explanation of the differences between the nurseries will do. It is not simply a matter of different methods and practices leading to different outcomes for children, or a matter of the social class of the intake of children.

Different circumstances and different values underpin the services which are provided for young children. As Cochran (1994, p. 627), who has investigated young children in wider comparative settings, has commented: 'Development is a complex multi-faceted process, so we are only likely to understand it if we look, not simply at patterns of non-parental care, but at the patterns of care in the context of other experiences, ideologies and practices.'

The much-quoted American psychologist Urie Bronfenbrenner (1979) has attempted to provide a theoretical framework for understanding such differences. He has suggested that to understand human development it is important to have an *ecological perspective*, and to examine how different interlocking contexts relate to one another – he specifies four interlocking levels or contexts. These are the microsystem (the most intimate settings in which a child is involved); the mesosystem (the inter-relationships between several intimate settings, e.g. home and nursery); the exosystem (the organizational settings which influence what the child experiences but in which he or she is not directly involved); and the macrosystem (the subculture or society). Many psychologists have argued that his four-level framework is too imprecise (Wachs, 1992). Explanations which draw on several different disciplines and epistemologies cannot be easily defined, nor easily studied within a single empirical framework. But Bronfenbrenner's ideas have generated a lot of interest in crosscultural studies of early years services, and there have been a number of recent books, such as Cochran's, which attempt to compare different countries, and match their socioeconomic status and cultural focus with the kind of childcare services which are provided. Bronfenbrenner argued that this is a legitimate use of his theory, to analyse systematically the differences between different settings, and to try to provide a taxonomy of those differences.

Bronfenbrenner used another key concept to describe the process of investigation, that of *ecological validity* – do the findings make sense to those people being investigated?: 'ecological validity refers to the extent to which the environment experienced by the subjects in a scientific experiment has the properties it is supposed or assumed to have by the investigator' (Bronfenbrenner, 1979, p. 29).

This principle of transparency and partnership, which is how I interpret 'ecological validity', has been an important consideration for me in undertaking this work. Whilst on the one hand people may not be able to stand back to see what they are doing in any wider context, and inevitably take many facets of their everyday circumstances for granted, on the other hand once this shift of viewpoint is presented to them, they must be able to recognize it. Otherwise, the study is diminished. I do not want to open the can of worms about the usefulness and relevance of research and how it is disseminated, problems which preoccupy policy-orientated researchers (Hammersley, 1993), but I hope this study will be relevant for those who were involved in it, and those who work in similar situations and enable them to identify aspects of practice, or of organization, which they may want to build on, develop or change. Certainly in the case of the UK nurseries, the study has happily been the starting point for the local authority in unravelling and changing the grim services which I described. How such changes have been carried out is another story.

Choosing the nurseries for the study

I have mentioned above that the choice of local authorities in each country was partly pragmatic – they were generous enough to fund the study. However there were some difficult decisions to be made in deciding what kind of nurseries to include in the study. In the regions of both Italy and Spain that I was investigating children aged 0–3 are part of the locally controlled education system. They then go on to full-time nursery classes, either free-standing or attached to primary school for a further two years, and start school when they are 5 or 6 years old as part of an annual September intake. Education and daycare provision cannot be easily separated – they are part of the same system. In the UK as I have already indicated, there are separate education and daycare systems, governed by different and incompatible legislative and administrative arrangements at a national and local level. The provision for children of working parents is mostly in the private and voluntary sector, and is for children aged 0–4 whose parents can afford to pay for it. Publicly funded daycare services are part of a welfare tradition for children in need. Nursery education is also publicly funded but is a separately administered and part-time service for children aged between 3 and 4 years, usually of no more than one year's duration – a nursery class or school is a place most children pass through briefly and rapidly. An additional complication in the UK is that in nursery education there is a built-in and insurmountable inequality of pay and conditions between those employed as teachers and those employed as nursery nurses or assistants, and I wanted to look at similar staff groups across the three countries.

Because of these discontinuities between care and education in the UK, I decided to focus the research on children aged 3 in publicly funded daycare because in some ways, although clearly not all, the provision is the most comparable across the three countries. The day nurseries are open for similar times, and the staff are permanently employed in them on standard and similar conditions of service, even though, in the UK, so few children are able to attend such nurseries. I looked at the similarities and differences in practice with these groups of 3-year-olds in the nurseries.

The nurseries themselves were chosen for me by local administrators in my sample local authorities as representing 'typical' practice. I explored the nurseries from a number of angles: from the point of view of the wider policy context, using local and national documentation; from the point of view of organization and staffing using questionnaires and attending meetings with staff; and through observations of staff and children using ethnomethodological methods, that is living the life of the nursery through the week.

Throughout the period of research I met regularly with administrators and other relevant professionals – for example educational psychologists – to relay back my findings, and to raise points about which I felt unclear or uncertain, either about policy or practice issues. At the end of my period of research in Italy and Spain, there was a conference for all the staff involved in which I tried to feed back my findings, and to debate them. In the UK this proved impossible to arrange, partly because there was a major restructuring of the social services department and the administrators themselves were transferred to other duties.

The background, personal and otherwise

The content of this book relates mainly to the findings of the research study I carried out over a period of one year. I have trawled the research literature to illustrate or contextualize or to provide an explanation for some of the findings. However I have also attended seminars and conferences, discussed issues, met those responsible for training nursery workers and visited nurseries over many years in both Spain and Italy; and as an ex-administrator, I have detailed knowledge of many day nurseries in the UK and of the legislation and policies which inform them and which determine their practice. This wider background knowledge necessarily frames what I write. No investigator is invisible and we all have opinions, however much we try to moderate them in the interests of rigorous inquiry and fair presentation of the facts. This reflexivity is a familiar theme in feminist or clinical literature but sits uncomfortably in the child development literature. I indulge in it, if that is the word, because it is less problematic than pretending to be absent from the account.

The book then focuses on the practices and circumstances of 12 nurseries, four in Italy, four in Spain and four in the UK. It aims to describe the differences between them in some detail, and to explain, as much as is possible, how these differences have occurred, and how different practices have come to be seen as 'normal'.

2

The Macrosystem: politics and policies in Italy, Spain and the UK

You can't understand anything unless you understand its relation to its context

(Arthur Miller)

There is already a great deal of information available about the history and systems of early childhood services in Italy, Spain and the UK. The European Childcare Network of the European Commission has provided useful summaries of services across member states. These are summarized in the consolidated report (1988), in subsequent annual reports and in the final publication of the network, *A Decade of Achievement* (1996). Each national 'expert' representative on the network has provided a comprehensive overview of services in his or her country, and has highlighted particular issues in the annual report and in specific briefing papers or in reports on particular topics.

There have also been a number of global crosscultural studies on childcare systems, which have included insightful accounts of services in Italy, Spain and the UK (Olmsted and Weikart, 1989; Lamb *et al.*, 1992; Cochran, 1993). In writing about Italy, for example, Corsaro and Emiliani (1992, p. 113) link the social and political history of Italy and the long tradition of city states and local autonomy, and the waxing and waning of the influence of the Catholic church, to the current uneven spread of services and regional variations across Italy, concluding that 'Italy has a history of progressive legislation and of poor implementation'.

All these studies and reports take as a starting point that social and political history inevitably determines the shape of early childhood services, and that the development of services can only be properly understood within such a framework. As Lamb *et al.* (1992, p. 12) confirm: 'The ease with which and the extent to which structural factors are translated into quality clearly vary depending on the culture, the context, and the alternative opportunities available to children, care providers and parents.' This chapter explores the contexts of the 12 nurseries investigated in this study. Because the information about wider national policies is easily available, I have only given a brief summary. Instead I focus on the local circumstances of each group of nurseries. These include the immediate geographical and demographic situation; the history of policy and provision and administration in the area; and on the climate of discussion and research which has been promoted in the local service. Again this information, particularly the demographic information, is not routinely comparable, but what is highlighted in each place serves to illustrate these local priorities.

It is also important to note that the conditions under which services are provided have changed continually. The nurseries in the Spanish and Italian cities in the study have been expanded and transformed in the last 20 or 30 years – whilst publicly funded services in the UK have contracted – although private services continue to expand in wealthier areas. But in all cases there have been – and continue to be – major political changes nationally and locally which affect the quality of the services delivered on the ground.

Summary of national policies

Italy

Women's participation in the labour force began to rise rapidly the 1970s, and several laws were passed at that time that addressed the rights of women workers. One of the most significant was Law 1044, passed in 1971, which recognized the right of any mother, working or not, to use state-supported day nurseries for their children who were less than 3 years of age. The *asilo nido* (literally, the nest) had been in existence as a model of care for working parents for some time, the first being established by a charity in 1831, but this law provided a more coherent rationale for developing them. Law 1044 set a national goal of achieving 3,800 *asili nidi* by 1976. This law was crucial in shifting perceptions of institutional care for young children.

The system of regional decentralization meant that regions could claim back from the state a substantial proportion of what they spent on the service. Whilst some regions, mainly in the south of Italy provided very little, other regions such as Emilia-Romagna fully exploited the opportunity to provide *asili nidi*.

Although at a state level the Ministry of Health was responsible for disbursing the money, some regions, like Emilia-Romagna, chose to locate the provision of *asili nidi* within an education framework. In the region 40% of children aged 0–3 have access to *asili nidi*, and about 95% of children aged 4–5 attend full-time nursery classes or schools. There is a negligible private sector; almost all provision is publicly funded and publicly run.

Spain

Spain suffered a considerable period of economic and social stagnation under the dictatorship of Franco, but by the 1970s there was a strong professional lobby to treat preschool services more seriously and to incorporate them fully into the education system. When the Socialist Party came to power in 1982 they incorporated some of these ideas, and from 1985 to 1990, the Ministry of Education undertook a process of systematic experimentation and consultation about new directions in education including preschool. This culminated in LOGSE, the Spanish Educational Reform Act, passed in 1990. This law makes the national Ministry of Education and departments of education in the autonomous communities with jurisdiction over education responsible for *all* services for children from 0 to 6, (*educacion infantil*). This first stage of education is subdivided into two cycles, 0–3 and 3–6, and education can be provided in nursery education in classes attached to schools for children 4–5, nurseries for children 0–6 (infant schools) and nurseries for children under 4. Children 3–6 have to be taught by trained teachers (and there have been changes in teacher training to enable specialization in working with children in *educacion infantil*). Children 0–3 have to have a trained teacher in charge, but there is discretion about the level of training of other workers. There is a very broad curriculum plan (Diseno Curricular Base) which stresses accountability to local communities. The framework for the curriculum 0–6 is set in LOGSE, but with considerable autonomy of interpretation at regional and commune level, and within the nurseries themselves, although at each level evidence of planning, monitoring and effectiveness is required. The broad aims of the service are that it should be 'child-centred, collaborative with parents, open towards the community and society'. These objectives are achieved 'through providing a stimulating and well resourced environment with professionally educated staff'. LOGSE also provided for the regulation and supervision of the private sector. Whilst LOGSE set a target for universal nursery education for children aged 3–5 by 1995 (mainly full time), targets for children 0–3 were left vague 'to satisfy demand' with no timetable. Some communes and regions have taken this seriously, most notably the commune of Madrid, which aims to provide for 25% of children 0–3; but others have provided relatively little.

UK

The UK has had a Conservative government since 1979, although at the time of writing an election is imminent. This government has had a long-standing commitment to regulating and cutting public expenditure, and in privatizing many services that were previously the domain of local authorities. Many local authority powers, including education powers, have been curtailed, and central government control of fiscal and legislative initiatives has become highly centralized. There is relatively little local autonomy.

The recent Education Reform Act omitted any mention of children before the statutory school age of 5. Nursery education exists but it does not feature in the most recent education legislation. There are places for approximately 26% of children. However 88% of these children attend on a part-time basis for between two and three hours per day. In the absence of nursery education, more than 50% of children aged 4 now attend regular school, in classes of 30 or more, with inadequate resources, a system much criticized by professionals. The government are now planning to withdraw almost all public funds from preschool provision, and instead to introduce vouchers given directly to parents of 4-year-olds which they may spend on private or public services as they choose.

The Children Act 1989 which the government has claimed is a great leap forward in the legal status of children, was primarily concerned with the reception of children into the care of the local authority, with a section on daycare uneasily added on to it. Its location has served to confirm the welfare status of publicly funded daycare provision. Publicly funded provision has in fact declined from offering places for just under 2% of children 0–5 to just under 1% since the Act was introduced. The Children Act also codified the regulation and inspection of private daycare, although there are also doubts whether this has had any material effect (Bull *et al.*, 1994). The services which provide for the largest number of children under compulsory school age are playgroups, which are usually parent run, are open between five and ten hours per week mainly in rented premises such as church halls, and which receive little or no public funds. Working mothers have to use private sector day nurseries, available only to those who can pay. The number of places has increased, at the same time as local authority places have shrunk (Table 2.1). Approximately 4.6% children under 5 attend such provision, and childminders cater for a further 7% of children under 5 whose parents are in work.

The Children Act stresses that the paramount consideration is 'the welfare of the child'. It also stresses the concept of 'parental responsibility' although it is not clear what this means in the context of daycare. It has no specific requirements for staff training or curriculum, and the guidance notes accompanying the Act contain only the general statement that 'the activities should be appropriate to age and developmental stage . . . there should be a variety so that children are given opportunities to develop physical, cognitive and social skills' (p. 32). The system in the UK is fragmented, poorly resourced and does not meet the most parsimonious estimates of demand.

Despite these differences in national policy, the rate of mothers in the labour force is now similar in each country. However there is a difference between the income levels of those who work and in the hours which are worked. In the UK, because of the unavailability of publicly funded or subsidized services, relatively few single parents are able to work. Those women who work full time come from predominantly professional two-earner families. A high percentage of women work part time (Figures 2.1 and 2.2). In the UK the income gap between rich and poor has been increasing, with a marked contrast between two-earner families and no-earner families. In Spain and Italy these patterns are reversed, and in Spain the gap between the poorest and richest has become narrower in the last ten years.

Summary of local policies and politics
Italy

It is worth stressing again the differences between local administration in the three countries. In Italy and Spain there is a three-tier system, but the nature of the tiers differs. In Italy I was looking

Table 2.1 Daycare places available in England for children under 8 as at 31 March – day nurseries, childminders and playgroups, 1985–95[1]

	Places in day nurseries				Places with childminders			Places in playgroups (part-time nursery groups)			
	Total	Local-authority provided[2]	Registered	Non-registered	Total	Local-authority provided[2]	Other registered persons	Total	Local-authority run[2]	Registered	Non-registered
1985	54,890	28,904	25,242	744	126,847	1,197	125,650	409,379	2,811	399,930	6,638
1986	57,659	28,920	27,923	816	137,732	1,544	136,188	412,391	2,641	403,224	6,526
1987	60,733	28,880	30,867	986	150,643	1,798	148,845	414,143	2,777	404,681	6,685
1988	66,237	28,951	36,252	1,034	163,700	1,659	162,041	409,063	2,572	401,173	5,318
1989	75,378	28,789	45,026	1,563	186,356	1,947	184,409	406,656	2,051	399,460	5,145
1990	87,451	27,978	57,669	1,804	205,567	1,889	203,678	416,381	2,045	409,563	4,773
1991	106,068	27,039	77,092	1,937	233,258	1,813	231,445	428,420	1,918	420,526	5,976
1992[3]	116,800	23,800	91,600	1,300	254,300	2,200	252,100	414,500	1,400	409,800	3,300
1993[3]	133,800	21,400	111,000	1,400	300,700	4,700	296,100	396,900	1,500	394,400	1,000
1994[3]	147,600	22,300	124,000	1,300	357,500	2,100	355,400	411,300	1,600	407,600	2,100
1995[3]	161,500	20,900	139,300	1,400	373,600	1,900	371,700	410,600	1,700	406,200	2,700

Notes:
1. Prior to 1992 data were collected for children aged under 5 only.
2. Includes facilities provided by voluntary organizations under agency arrangements, under Section 22 of the National Health Service Act 1946.
3 These figures have been rounded to the nearest 10 or 100 as appropriate. Figures may not add to totals because of rounding.
Source: Department of Health, 1996.

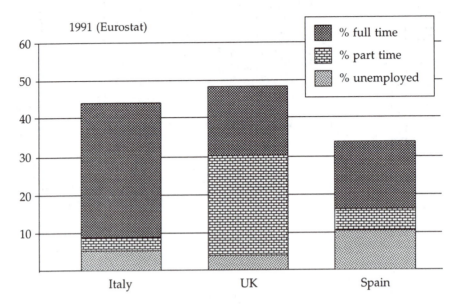

Figure 2.1 Mothers of children 0–16 in employment

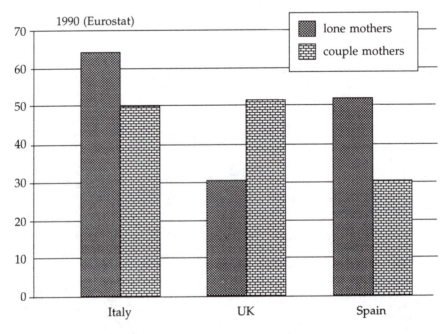

Figure 2.2 Employment: lone and couple mothers

at several communes in one region – Emilia-Romagna. The communes or districts within Emilia-Romagna, many of which, like the region itself, were communist or in the control of the left, are responsible for providing the services, and liaise closely with the region in doing so. I was working in three communes within Emilia-Romagna, representing one large city and two smaller towns. The city had many tourists, but the towns had few. All these places were wealthy, and contained few visible signs of poverty. Much old housing, including Renaissance buildings, had been renovated for general habitation. New public housing schemes were socially mixed and residence in them was not generally an indication of low income, nor did their inhabitants require special compensatory welfare services as in the UK. The four Italian nurseries were sited in pleasant residential areas on the outskirts of the city and towns. The nurseries were integrated into local policy-making, and senior officials and politicians took a lively interest in the service.

The region and the communes provide detailed demographic data. In 1987, the most recent year for which figures were provided in the communes, the per capita income (household income figures were not available) was approximately £6,730 per annum (on today's figures approximately £11,000 per annum). As 16% of the population were either under 14 or over 65, the median figure for per capita income is likely to be much higher, and that for actual earnt income higher still. An estimated 4.6% were unemployed. Almost as many women as men were in the workforce. Of those in work, approximately 11% were employed in agriculture, 37% in industry and 52% in service industries. Social indicators, such as expenditure on cinemas, sport, theatre and other entertainment amounted to about 13% of income. The communes were homogeneous, and the inward and outward migration figures were less than 2% per annum. These were very prosperous stable communities, well provided with services of all kinds. The region has had an impressive history in developing and supporting nurseries and the service is widespread. The principles of the service are defined as

- recognition of children's rights as members of society, and therefore the attention placed upon their cognitive, emotional and social development;
- major participation by parents in the life and activity of the services; and

- the importance of the skill and professionalism of staff members reached through continuous training courses.

The region has instigated and supported many research projects both directly and indirectly, with universities and research institutes, which have led directly to developments in services. La Nuova Italia imprint, based in the nearby town of Firenze, had published a series of books on the history and practice of nurseries, or *asili nidi*, which were widely known and distributed. The local research institute, IRPA, had its own imprint and had similarly published a number of local studies and reviews. In particular they had reviewed the role of the co-ordinators, the trainer-administrators for the nurseries – who are discussed in Chapter 4. The communes had published their own guides on the use of resources, and some of the nurseries had worked with the co-ordinators to produce videos on aspects of everyday life at the nursery, for discussion with parents, staff and others. The local universities have also undertaken research into activities at the nurseries and their work is well known in international journals (Emiliani and Zani, 1984; Corsaro and Emiliani, 1992). One of the communes in the region, Reggio Emilia – which was not included in this study – has achieved worldwide recognition for the quality of its nursery provision, and Malaguzzi, the person for many years in charge of the programme, has achieved worldwide renown for his educational views (Malaguzzi, 1993). The nurseries participated in a lively and continuous research programme, and the findings of the research were continually disseminated and discussed. Despite turbulent national politics, and although there have been some new financial restrictions, the region and the communes within it are continually developing their practice and experimenting with new services.

Spain

In Spain there is also a three-tier system. The region of Catalonia is an autonomous region of Spain with considerable powers regarding education; unlike the region of Emilia-Romagna it is also a direct service provider. The official language is Catalan, and there is considerable sponsorship of Catalan linguistic and cultural events. However the region is nationalist, and the political perspective is to the right of centre, although for the past term of office, the Catalan nationalists have supported the Socialist government. Catalonia has taken a low profile in sponsoring developments in early childhood services. The nurseries provided by the region are generally considered of a lower standard than those provided by Barcelona, in terms of staffing ratios and other conventional measures.

The research was based in Barcelona, the biggest municipality of the region. Like the region they also take considerable pride in Catalan language and culture, and consider it an important aspect of the service they provide. Barcelona is a thriving cosmopolitan city and has a very substantial tourist trade. It presents extremes of wealth and poverty, and there is a legacy from the time of Franco of peripheral housing estates serving the low paid, which present acute problems. Despite this, as a city, it is relatively socially cohesive, perhaps because of the emphasis on Catalan culture. Although it has attracted many workers from outside the city, mainly from the south of Spain but also some north African, they are expected to integrate into this culture.

The ten subdistricts of the city each have their own demographic profile. Three of the four Spanish nurseries were in lively mixed inner-city areas; one was in a residential district. There has been much renovation of inner-city properties and one of the nurseries was created out of the end of a terrace of worker cottages. Unemployment is relatively low overall at about 10%. About 50% of women are in the workforce.

Barcelona has had a left-wing local government, and has chosen to take a very high profile in developing the early childhood services, which they provide directly. About 8% of the eligible population of children 0–3 is in publicly funded day nurseries, a number which is gradually increasing, although the number in private provision is estimated to be higher. The chairwoman of the Education Committee, an ex-MP and now a senator, and a highly respected intellectual, had a strong personal interest in the nurseries for children 0–3, and had spoken and written about the service on many occasions. As in Italy, the service was integrated with other aspects of local government. Nurseries were linked to one of the ten subdistricts of the city, and had a nominal voice at least in local education policy-making forums and planning. The service has been expanding rapidly, and all aspects of the service – training, resources, curriculum and research and development – were continually discussed and reviewed in order to inform the next stage of expansion. The volume of research and documentation is not so extensive as in Emilia-Romagna, and is not well known internationally outside Spanish-speaking countries, but it is considerable nevertheless. A leading role in articulating issues and disseminating material has been played by Rosa Sensat, a professional association of infant teachers, which has links with other similar organizations throughout Spain, and which publishes a monthly magazine to keep members up to date on current issues. Rosa Sensat has a substantial library on early childhood and runs its own training courses including an annual summer school to which leading psychologists and early years teachers are invited to contribute. The nurseries were also encouraged to develop their own training programmes – referred to again in the next chapter.

The UK

The UK city, which for reasons which will become obvious is not named, is in the north of England. It is smaller than Barcelona, but bigger than any of the Italian communes. It was a thriving industrial city, but the largest firms, which employed many thousands of workers, have shut down, and the levels of male unemployment are extremely high. The local authority which was also socialist had watched the decline in industry and break-up of communities in dismay, but although there were small ameliorative schemes financed through various urban funding initiatives, the local authority was relatively powerless to influence events, partly because of the centralist government who have exercised tight control over local finances.

The city had a long history of public housing but such housing had catered mainly for low-paid manual workers, and housing is in effect socially segregated. In some cases the estates were built to offer cheap housing for employees of factories that had since closed. In these areas of public housing where major industries have closed down it is commonplace to see boarded-up or gutted houses, ubiquitous graffiti, litter, broken glass and wrecks of cars. The shops that are still open are barred with steel shutters. Although the 1991 census returns for the city as a whole suggest that 5.5% of families are single-parent households, and 4.3% of households have three or more children, local officials claim that single-parent families with large numbers of children are prominent on these public housing estates as a subcultural phenomena: having a large family is an occupation when no other is available; and men can still show 'manliness' in fathering children when they have no other function as wage-earners. Low manual wage rates and the complexities of the taxation and benefit system mean that even if they wished to work, and work was available, many young parents are better off on benefit than in work. All the day nurseries in the English city were located on such bleak housing estates.

Of the population of the city, 18% were under 14, a much higher percentage than in Italy (where the combined percentage of under 14 and over 65 was 16%). Of households, 35% lived in council accommodation, and 69% of those were unemployed or in receipt of housing benefit because they could not afford the full rent. Some 34% of all families with children were in receipt of free school meals and other welfare benefits although in the areas where the nurseries were situated this was in excess of 90% in some schools. The registered unemployment rate for the city as a whole was 18.6% although this varied from district to district. The *household* cash income of a family on benefit depends on the number of adults and children, but for a single-parent family with three children could be less than £5,000 per annum. In some of the areas where the nurseries were situated, the unemployment rates were in excess of 40%. A local study of one of these areas suggested that the level of male unemployment was 50%, and of those in employment, most were in unskilled manual occupations. In this area twice as many women were likely to be employed as men, but mainly in part-time low-skilled occupations such as cleaning or waitressing. In the city as a whole there were no figures available for inward and outward migration but approximately 4% of the population were from minority ethnic groups, of whom the majority were from the Indian subcontinent.

Nursery education for 3- and 4-year-olds was available for about 50% of children, although as elsewhere, most of this was part time. Some of the nursery education practice was distinguished and widely respected. There were practitioners with a national reputation who had contributed to Open University programmes and to teacher training programmes at the local university, although there was little local research and no locally produced materials.

Most of the provision was in the private and voluntary sector, in playgroups and in a few non-profit community or voluntary nurseries. Private sector nurseries, although still small in number, were increasing, catering for just under 2% of children aged 0–4.

At the time of the study the day nurseries were almost invisible as a local service. They provided places for just over 1% of children aged 0–4. They had been seen as a minor aspect of social services welfare provision, as one of a number of therapeutic services aimed at restoring damaged family life – an uphill task under the circumstances. At the time the study commenced there had been no recent or sustained investment in terms of resources, curriculum or research, although the nurseries were able to call on the services of the educational psychology service for assessment of children and advice on handling them in individual cases. The psychologists also offered a limited amount of in-house training. In the past some of the nursery teachers had attempted to work with the day nurseries in developing curricular ideas, but these attempts had foundered, and only one member of staff in the day nursery sample made any reference to them. One of the nurseries had had a very brief one-off training in the use of 'High Scope' methods, but again this limited initiative had petered out. There was no written information of any kind about the nature of the service which was provided, nor was there any perceived need to provide it. The Children Act 1989 had required the city to produce for the first time a list of all services available for children under 5, but no information was given on the kind of service being offered other than the barest details of numbers of places available and opening hours – mostly part time. The day nurseries at that time were a neglected, underutilized and isolated service, and their neglect mirrored the wider national picture of declining numbers and a dearth of information or research.

Bronfenbrenner (1979) coined the phrase 'the empty setting' to describe how nurseries appear in much of the research literature. But nurseries are sited in particular locations, and they have their own organizational culture, partly determined by what happens outside, and partly by what goes on inside. This chapter has attempted to fill in some of the broader picture and has described some of the wider conditions and systems which influence nursery provision. The 12 nurseries were operating in very different contexts and serving very different populations. The next chapter looks at who works in them.

3

Staffing

We must know that children, although naturally inclined, do not acquire the art of becoming friends or teachers of one another by finding models in heaven or in manuals; rather, children extract and interpret models from adults, when the adults know how to work, discuss, think, research and live together

(Loris Malaguzzi)

Who works in nurseries? How are they trained? What sort of conditions do they work under? How do they view themselves and their job? These are the questions I set out to explore.

The information collected

I tried to get a rounded picture of the staff who were working in the nurseries. I collected job descriptions where they existed and inquired about interview and selection procedures for staff. In Italy I sat in on the 'concourse' – the competitive examination system for public posts. Over 100 applicants, those who had been the most successful in the written examination, were briefly interviewed for vacant nursery posts over a period of two days. The interviews were undertaken by a panel of experts, made up of an academic, a trades union official and a local administrator. The panel met at one end of a vast sixteenth-century hall beautifully decorated with renovated frescos. They had their leisurely lunch break in a local restaurant whose home-made pasta was beyond compare – the local speciality was a zucchini-filled ravioli! The rituals and the settings of the appointments procedure, and the absence of any involvement of nursery staff themselves, were extremely surprising for me, used to the utilitarian procedures in the UK, but recruitment to public services here, as in some other countries, is an auspicious occasion, a ceremonious rite of passage.

I constructed what I hoped was a translation-proof questionnaire for staff, which I piloted in Italy and the UK. One hundred and twenty-eight staff in all the sample nurseries completed the questionnaire. I drew on some of the ideas of Richman and McGuire (1988) and asked staff to rank various aspects of their work but I included in addition a series of questions about how staff related to each other, and about the levels of their job satisfaction. I stressed that the staff questionnaires were confidential and I would not disclose the source of any personal information or comments. For some staff this was not a sufficient guarantee, and in one of the UK nurseries a few of the staff offered to talk to me as a group about the questionnaire, but would not fill in individual forms.

In each nursery in Italy and Spain I tried to establish, with the help of the translator, how often staff meetings were held, and to what extent they constituted a decision-making forum. I attended a staff meeting in each nursery, with the translator in tow. I noted who participated in the meetings and on what basis; if there were informal hierarchies if not formal ones.

The staff questionnaire included questions about the way in which staff related to one another, and I tried to supplement these questions through observations of staff. The American rating scale of childcare as a work environment assumes that such 'collegiality' is an important factor in determining the smooth running of the nursery (Jorde-Bloom, 1988). Getting on with work colleagues, being able to share ideas and experiences, giving and receiving support, enhance how staff are able to undertake their work with the children. There are exercises designed to improve such collegiality, which in English jargon is called 'team-building' (Rodd, 1994). This collegiality is both formal and informal. So as well as the questionnaires and team meetings and the observations in the rooms, I joined in on staff mealtimes and lunch breaks, and attended various social functions that were held whilst I was working in the nurseries: a sale of work; an evening party; a fête.

I observed staff whilst they were with the children. As I describe later in the section on children, observation as a method has its limits, quite apart from the difficulties of deciding what to watch and how to categorize it. Observation is an uncomfortable phenomenon for both observer and observed. It is an odd convention to pretend to be invisible and watch other people work. It breaks all the usual social rules. Some of the staff were used to researchers and observers in the nursery and were familiar with the procedure; but a few of the staff I tried to observe could not accommodate to being watched and were highly self-conscious about my presence.

The question of feedback to those being observed is also an issue. I was frequently asked by staff 'What did you notice?' 'What have you seen?' I tried to be as open as I could about my observations; but in any case in order to interpret the meaning of some of what I had observed I had to discuss incidents with staff. In other words, it is impossible to be a neutral observer, and one's own subjective impressions, the social context and the ease of those being observed all influence what is seen.

The observation of practice was sometimes ethically problematic. The overwhelming majority of practice in all settings was caring, but on a few occasions I saw practice which was so far from the norm within the local authority group of nurseries which I was investigating that I felt concerned. I did not intervene but I raised the issue as soon as possible with the member of staff whom I had observed, and asked in a neutral way, and as part of a number of queries, if she could describe what she had been doing at that time. Since the staff members I spoke to had self-convincing rationales for their actions, and did not perceive them as problematic, I then raised the issue with administrators – whose job it was to define and oversee the practice – in my feedback sessions with them. In a very few instances for various reasons the administrators were unable to agree or take any action.

Ball (1993, p. 32) has ironically described this kind of ethnographical approach as 'soft data and the skilful self':

> Not only do researchers have to go into unknown territory, they must go unarmed . . . with no interview schedules or observation procotols to stand between them and the raw real. They stand alone with their individual selves. They themselves are the primary research tool with which they must find, identify, and collect the data. They must charm the respondents into co-operation. They must learn to blend or pass in the research setting, put up with the boredom and hours of an empty notebook, cringe in the face of faux pas made in front of those whose co-operation they need, and engage in the small deceptions and solve the various ethical dilemmas which crop up in most ethnographies.

Composition of the workforce

I obtained background information about the staff make-up: ages, gender, marital status, level of training, pay and conditions of service and length and type of service.

The staff questionnaires suggest that the staff groups are sur-prisingly similar across the 12 nurseries and across the three coun-tries. Almost all the staff are women. About 5% of staff in Barcelona are men, and two men were included in the Spanish group in the sample (in some other parts of Spain the percentage of men employed is higher than in Barcelona). The percentage of men is negligible in Italy, partly due to Law 444, passed in 1968, which insisted on an all-female workforce. Although opposed by the unions, and subsequently modified, this legislation may have influenced career perceptions. At any rate, there was only one man in the Italian sample, and he was regarded by his colleagues as highly unusual. There was also one man in the UK sample (who has subsequently left), where the employment of men was gener-ally regarded as problematic because of concerns about child abuse, a point explored further in the next chapter.

The employment of men is an issue for a number of reasons. First, as with any gender-biased work, it is an equal opportuni-ties issue; under European legislation men and women in theory should have equal access to any job and equal treatment within it. Second, the gendered nature of early childhood services con-firms stereotypes about it being a woman's job to look after young children rather than viewing it as a task to be shared equally between men and women. The gendered nature of caring profes-sions, and the consequences to women in terms of lower pay and conditions, is currently under investigation by the OECD (Christopherson, 1997). Third, there is an argument that for chil-dren themselves it is a limiting experience to be looked after only by women; a wider familiarity with role models and gender expectations would broaden their upbringing, particularly for those children from single-parent families. This presupposes that men do indeed bring something different to the task of looking after children besides their physical presence. Making generaliza-tions about the nature of men and 'male role models' is surely as difficult an enterprise as making generalizations about what women do.

Whatever the caveats, in Barcelona and Emilia-Romagna strate-gies were being developed to improve men's access; in the English city, in so far as there were any deliberate strategies to develop the service, men's access was in effect discouraged.

As well as gender patterns, there were other common features of the workforce. About two thirds of the staff had children of their own. A small minority of staff were single parents. Almost

all staff had some form of basic qualification (although as discussed below, this differed considerably between countries). The
average age of the staff in all the nurseries (excluding ancillary
workers) was between 30 and 40 years. The average length of
service in each nursery was between 4 and 12 years. The workers
in Spain were slightly older and had been in their posts slightly
longer, but not significantly so. In all the nurseries the staff were
experienced and formed a relatively stable group. Because of this
stability, it was hard for newly qualified staff to find a post and
it was unusual to find a member of staff under 25 years of age in
any nursery.

As described above, in Italy, entrance to the profession was by
public concourse. The staff at the individual nurseries had no say
in who was allocated to them. In practice, very few people were
appointed directly from the concourse. Only a small percentage
were successful, and they were almost all allocated to supply
posts, where they were likely to remain for several years. A similar
system operated in Spain. In the UK there was no public examination and interviews were more personalized, with the person
in charge of each nursery having a key role. But even in the UK
there were many more applicants than jobs available. The effect
was to depress mobility.

A third to half of the staff in each country had little or no experience of nursery work other than in the nursery in which they
were working. This lack of turnover in publicly funded daycare
is in striking contrast to figures given for the private market in
the USA and UK, where turnover is 50% per annum or more
(Phillips *et al.*, 1991; Penn, 1994a).

Pay and conditions

Spain and Italy

All staff, except those on supply, had secure pensionable jobs. The
basic rate of pay was roughly similar in each country, although
whereas the increments in Spain and Italy were for length of
service, in the UK the pay was linked to level of seniority as well
as to length of service and the range was far greater, with a starting salary of £8,266 to a top salary for a long-serving officer in
charge of £21,357. The conditions varied considerably. In Italy and
Spain staff worked a 36-hour week, of which six hours was non-
contact time. There were usually two shifts, either a morning shift

beginning at 7.30 or 8 a.m. and an afternoon shift ending at 5 or 6 p.m., with an overlap from 10 or 11 to about two. Lunchtimes for staff were usually sociable and communal affairs – with excellent fresh food – held whilst the children were taking an afternoon nap. The staff often ate in the kitchen, which in the newer nurseries were designed for eating in. The staffrooms in the Spanish nurseries were well equipped with up-to-date professional materials, books, journals, photographic and written records and videos; the Italian nurseries less so.

All these nurseries closed down entirely for August and for a week or so at Christmas and Easter – the holiday allocation was slightly more generous in Italy than in Spain – 34 paid days as against 30 days. Adult:child ratios varied with the age of the child and with the time of day. Group size and age banding were regarded as important as ratios. Children under 1 year of age were in groups of no more than six. Usually two or three staff would be allocated to a group, and all would be on duty at the peak activity time in the morning, but only one or two members of staff at the beginning and end of the day. Cover arrangements varied slightly, but supply staff were almost always available.

The UK

In the UK staff worked a 39-hour week. The nurseries did not close except for bank holidays, and staff had 20–25 days holiday entitlement depending on length of service. These holidays had to be negotiated according to the rotas, which considerably complicated the organization of the nursery. In theory all staff time was supposed to be direct contact time with children. There was no non-contact time set aside for training or personal development. The shifts, usually three separate shifts, varied so that in theory staff ratios could always be maintained at the same level. I stress 'in theory' because there was often a difference between the organizational requirements and the actual practice, between what people thought and said they were doing and what they actually did. I return to this point below.

In these UK nurseries there was very little time for the staff to be together with one another, either to compare and discuss experiences or to socialize. Staff were required to eat with the children, and by comparison with the highly sociable mealtimes in Italy and Spain, for both staff and children lunchtimes were often dismal affairs with poor food and little attention to presentation or any kind of social rituals. The primary function of the English meal-times, according to the manager of the service, was to nourish malnourished children and make sure they ate one solid meal rather than to celebrate the variety of tastes or textures or any other aspect of the food. Anthropologists such as Levi-Strauss (1968) and Goody (1982) argue that all humans have in common that they use language and cook food, and just as people can be grouped by languages, so cultures can be distinguished by the time they spend and the importance they accord to the prepara-tion and consumption of food. In the UK nurseries, mealtimes could be described as grim and dutiful fuelling. Two of the cooks were lively and committed women, with articulate views about the service they were providing, but the culture of the nursery and the meagre budget were against them. In two of those nurs-eries meals for the children consisted of one course with an emphasis on fast turn-around and tidy eating and avoidance of mess; and the staff either ate under these conditions or had a packed lunch consumed singly and separately.

After the children's lunchtime the staff would escape for a brief half-hour break according to their rota turn, and retreat to the staffroom. All the nurseries had staffrooms, but these were barren rooms – they contained few if any professional materials, perhaps a book, most likely a magazine or a mail-order catalogue. One staffroom possessed as a reference book *Common Sense in the Nursery* by a Mrs Sydney Frankenburg, dated 1934. It had been the property of a previous matron and had lain untouched for many years. Its opening paragraph is a diatribe about feeding by the clock:

> The most important point, apart from the food itself, about infant feeding is absolute regularity . . . Infants who are fed at irregular hours stand a very poor chance of acquiring efficient gastric func-tions, for the centres which control these functions must be trained in regular and periodic habits, so that when they are working they may work their best, and when they are at rest they may have ample opportunities for recovery.
>
> (*Ibid.*, p. 15)

The book is a neat illustration both of how little reference sources are consulted, and of how much ideas about practice are derived from the fashions and fads of the time.

Since there was a low level of occupancy by children, for a variety of reasons, and since the ratios required under the terms of the Children Act (interpreted as 1:3 for children 2 and under; 1:5 for children aged 2–3; 1:8 for children aged 3–5 at all times) were much more generous than in Italy or Spain, the nurseries appeared somewhat overstaffed by comparison. In one nursery, the number of staff exceeded the numbers of children for certain periods in the day.

Ancillary staff

All the nurseries had ancillary staff to help with domestic and janitorial duties, but the status and roles of these workers differed between nurseries and between countries. In the Italian nurseries the staff had 'helpers' known as *dade*. Corsaro and Emiliani (1992) argue that *dade* are best seen as surrogate grandmothers, although in the sample nurseries they were mostly younger women. The *dade* help with mealtimes, serving and cleaning up, and sometimes take on other supportive roles, assisting in the rooms. The nurseries all had cooks, usually two, and cleaners. They might also have laundrywomen. Janitation and gardening were undertaken by the commune. The administration, secretarial and financial work was undertaken centrally by the commune.

The Spanish nurseries had fewer ancillary staff. Each nursery had two cooks, a reflection of the importance accorded to food, and a domestic. But staff shared out other roles between themselves – helping clear up the rooms, maintaining the flowers in the courtyards and taking on any small jobs which required sorting out. The local authority had devolved most of the secretarial, financial and administrative work to the nursery, and each nursery elected one of its members as a full-time secretary to undertake such work.

The UK nurseries had one cook, sometimes with a part-time assistant, and a cleaner. The gardens were irregularly maintained by the local authority. All the secretarial work was undertaken by the officer in charge and her deputy, both of whom were supernumerary. This secretarial work was very time-consuming because of the nature of the admissions procedure, where careful and ongoing consideration had to be given to the times individual children were attending, and constant juggling of the attendance packages was necessary. The two most senior and expensive staff in the nursery were therefore primarily concerned with administrative tasks rather than with considerations of practice. There was little budgetary autonomy, and most of the financial resources were tightly controlled by the local authority.

Organization

The most striking differences in the staff groups concerned organization and training. These aspects were related. The emphasis on training and development both determined and reflected the organization of the nurseries.

The nurseries in Italy and Spain were organized collectively, in the UK hierarchically. In the Anglo-American literature the concepts of management and leadership are so embedded in the understanding of the organization of work that it is almost impossible to envision an alternative way of thinking about how tasks in a work setting can be identified, prioritized, distributed and undertaken other than by having a hierarchical system in which managers or leaders direct and control (and perhaps inspire) the flow of work.

Most of the rhetoric about management and leadership omits to mention money and status. Managers get paid more, and have more power over decision-making; the other side of the coin is that non-managers get paid less and have less power over decision-making. Non-managers have to defer to managers; they are subordinate to them, and their status and remuneration are less. The pathways to becoming a manager are embodied in the notion of a 'career structure' that is a delineation of the steps – promotion – towards the goal of becoming a manager. This career structure, the possibility, rather than the promise, of gaining more control, more prestige and more money in a work setting is held out as an incentive towards doing your job well. If you perform well you can think about applying for promotion although of course you may not get it, and may become embittered if you do not.

Within early years in the Anglo-American literature these concepts of management and leadership have been adopted uncritically. The literature assumes that hierarchical management is a 'given' and focuses instead on what attributes successful managers possess. Richman and McGuire (1988) for instance suggest that successful managers are those who involve themselves directly in day-to-day activities, and who are seen to be expert practitioners. Jorde-Bloom (1988) has produced an Early

Childhood Work Environment Rating Scale. She delineates 10 areas in which staff can rate the nursery in which they work, but implicit in this scale is the notion of a manager or director. Rodd (1994) has written a book *Leadership in Early Childhood Education*, looking at nurseries in Australia. She concludes (*ibid.* p. 14) that 'The development of Leadership skills is a vital and critical challenge for early childcare professionals . . . if the provision of socially and culturally responsive services for young children and their families is to be successful in the next century'. Hierarchy is also implicit although not explicit in this account. In the Anglo-American literature on nurseries the idea of a hierarchical organization of work is pervasive. There were a few attempts to consider alternative ways of working in the 1960s and 1970s but these were very self-conscious efforts and petered out (Stanton 1989).

In a number of European countries however there are enduring and long-standing co-operative traditions in nurseries. Saraceno (1977) considers that these derive from the radical experiments of the 1960s, but there is also evidence that the traditions are much older and more culturally widespread (Corsaro and Emiliani, 1992). In Spain they relate back to the worker schools of the 1930s; in northern Italy to the agricultural co-operatives. Whatever their origins, the nurseries in Spain and Italy in this sample were organized as collectives, that is all teacher/care staff were paid similar rates, no one was in charge and decision-making was collectively undertaken.

In Italy the collective nurseries had some but not a great deal of autonomy, and key administrative and professional/training decisions were taken by the co-ordinators or by other administrators. The co-ordinators are each responsible for a group of 8–10 nurseries. They are well qualified, with a degree or postgraduate degree as well as having practical experience in the field. Often they have undertaken research in collaboration with a local university or research institute. The region had assisted the communes to finance an extension of the co-ordinator system, and this expansion had been monitored by the local research institute, IRPA. The co-ordinators are in effect the managers of the nurseries. They have a key role in support and development of the service; they advise on policy, they have overall responsibility for the administration, they make sure professional standards are met and they play a key role in training and in research. However they are not based in the nurseries and on a day-to-day basis the nurseries run themselves co-operatively. There were no supernumary posts in the Italian nurseries and everyone took a share in greeting parents, answering the phone, etc.

In Spain, the nurseries have more autonomy. There were only four co-ordinators for all the nurseries in the city, and they had a role which could be described as a mixture of support and troubleshooting. They knew the nurseries well but would only intervene in exceptional circumstances. The nurseries were responsible for their own administration, their own training and development plans, and their own professional standards. They elected a supernumary member of staff as a secretary to deal with all administrative issues, but when I asked about their work these secretaries were at pains to point out that they were in no way 'in charge' and decision-making was firmly collective.

The collective way of working meant that the activities and professional development of the nursery were conceived of as a whole for the nursery. The nursery itself was viewed as a functioning organism, as opposed to a collection of individuals in the same place. Rather like the way in which hierarchy was viewed as implicit in the Anglo-American context, collectivism was taken for granted in the Italian and Spanish contexts. It was not problematic *per se*.

The view expressed informally in the discussions that I had prior to undertaking the research was that relationships between staff were an important model for children's relationships with each other, and the more egalitarian the relationships between staff, the more the children would develop reciprocal friendships and co-operation amongst themselves. This link between staff organization and child behaviour did not feature in any of the official documentation, although in discussions and on the questionnaires the Spanish staff, in particular, were thoughtful and volunteered many comments about their collective way of working:

> I have the good luck to be in a team where I have observed few conflicts, where people talk about things, a kind of dialogue which makes conflict unnecessary. Also we have a lot of freedom within the group rooms and within the framework set by the nursery.

> Even if I didn't like the work I would still like my colleagues. Bad relationships with colleagues would spread to work with the children.

I'm in agreement with the structure and organization of the centre although from a practical point of view, working and deciding as a team takes longer, and things get done more slowly. Even so, I would not change it even if certain aspects of punctuality and organization are lacking.

Working in a team is positive but difficult – you have to take account of a range of views and arrive at the best compromise agreement.

We need to find a form of organization that recognizes all aspects and all the diversity of a team.

We have differences but they are not sources of conflict. Perhaps the fact that we have enough autonomy and we have friendships within the group means we have very few conflicts.

As in all work situations there were some dissenters who did not share in the general perceptions:

If people would behave decently, everything could be sorted out.

Our meetings are disorganized, and we do not have enough time for room meetings.

In Italy, in two of the nurseries there appeared to be a problem with the administration, which as a temporary visitor, I could not fully explore or understand. The staff expressed resentment towards the administration and this overshadowed all other comments about staff organization:

I have the recurring impression that the administration undervalues our commitment and professionalism and the seriousness with which we try to carry out our work.

It's too bureaucratic and it has got more so over the years.

In the other nurseries, although dialogue and co-operation with colleagues were valued, none of the staff made any general comments about the value of collective organization as the Spanish staff did, possibly because their method of working was in fact less autonomous.

The UK nurseries were organized in a hierarchical fashion. There was a manager of the service, who was in turn managed by an assistant director of social services. There was an officer in charge (OIC) and her deputy, both supernumary. Then there were a number of graded or senior posts, and the remainder of the staff were employed on basic grades. Altogether there were nine grades. Although there were some team meetings these did not deal with administrative decisions and were not used for allocating work between staff. Since the nurseries were open throughout the year, rotas had to be continually reorganized to allow for cover of staff who were absent on holiday or away sick. This meant that the whole group of staff were rarely present, and organizing meetings was still more difficult.

Instead of any group discussion of professional progress there was a system known as 'supervision' in which each member of staff was allocated half an hour every fortnight or so to talk with a more senior member of staff about the problems she was encountering in her daily practice. Again there was no explicit rationale for this practice; it was something that everyone did without it being made clear why or what it was intended to achieve, and because it was embedded, it was difficult to explain to an outsider. One OIC explained that 'Staff are encouraged to openly air their feelings in staff supervision'. But staff airing their personal problems put themselves in a difficult position in relation to their boss, because the person to whom they were airing their grievance was also likely to be the person who had caused it. In this particular nursery some of the staff felt angry that the OIC and her deputy spent little time in the rooms and were unaware of the difficulties the staff encountered, but had been unable to air these feelings in supervision. Moreover any problem or grievance was first perceived as a personal rather than as a collective problem.

Because 'supervision' and individual personal contact were favoured over group discussion as a means of resolving problems and developing practice there was little group debate about anything other than trivial issues, and any decisions had to be ratified by going up the lines of hierarchy, or proceeded by instructions sent down through them. The minutes of the monthly meetings of the service manager with the OICs focused on such bureaucratic items as the use of rectal medication; nomination of a shop steward; details of a new clerical assistant at headquarters; overspend on provisions budget; and issuing of leaflets on complaints procedures. In the time I was present, and from what I could ascertain from past minutes, there were no discussions about practice – what the nursery workers were actually doing with the children.

In the nurseries the comments made by staff were within the context of this framework of hierarchy, and related to whether or not the boss or 'management' liked and respected their work. In the first instances quoted the OIC was clearly respected by her staff; but in the others there was more ambiguity:

> I feel I am respected as a professional by my supervisor and colleagues.

> We have an honest co-operative staff and management working together.

> There should be more consultation with staff over admissions.

> Management should spend more time in the group rooms.

> The senior staff should consult more with others.

Some of the OICs in turn felt they were having to spend their time on petty secretarial and administrative duties, rather than being involved in and leading practice:

> At times I feel like a junior clerk but recognize as a manager this is a necessary part of the job.

> I wish there was less administration and I didn't have to spend so much time ordering fish-fingers.

In each country the form of organization of the nursery differed considerably. This in turn led to differences in the way training was conceived, valued and translated into practice.

Training

Training is usually taken to mean initial or basic training; but it is widely recognized in many fields that postqualification training, the continuous or in-service training which is provided, is a key means of keeping up to date and improving and developing practice.

In Italy initial training programmes and requirements are confusing. Although staff working in *asili nidi* are now termed *educatori* the law still permits anyone holding one of three qualifications to work in an *asilo nido*: *diploma di puericultrice*, a one-year course; and *diploma di viglatrice d'infanzia* and *diploma di assistant d'infanzia*, both three-year courses. In addition some staff have a *magistrale*, a three to four-year post-16 qualification similar in length and type to that of a nursery school teacher. A majority of those in the case study nurseries possessed a *magistrale* qualification; the rest were mainly *assistante*. A few had degrees, in psychology or sociology. One was an ex-secondary-school science teacher.

In Spain the opportunities for formal training in nursery work under Franco had been limited, but because of LOGSE, a tremendous impetus had been given to providing a standardized in-service-based training qualification as a teacher in early education 0–6. In Barcelona a mainly unqualified workforce had in the space of five-years become 80% qualified as teachers. Again there were a few members of staff with degrees in psychology, or in one case fine art, but they were required also to have a teaching certificate. The teaching qualification aimed to provide students with

- an intellectual base, an ability to abstract, deduce and synthesize;
- a background of pedagogy and psychology; and
- a thorough knowledge of health and hygiene.

In both Spain and Italy one sixth of the working week was non-contact time, for training, personal development and organizational matters. Post-qualification training was seen as a collective rather than as a personal responsibility. Any team meetings, or training meetings put on by the commune came out of this time. In Italy, the training sessions were mainly organized by the co-ordinators. The researchers at IRPA suggested that within the *asilo nidi* three styles or models of teaching could be identified, which they named as transmission, phenomenological and dialectic. The transmission model is the traditional educational curricular approach in which a codified amount of knowledge or subject matter is transmitted to the children by the teacher, and the pedagogic mission is to code and define the knowledge which is to be passed on. The phenomenological approach took the view that knowledge was complex, multifaceted and non-hierarchical, and in transmitting the knowledge the teacher had to take account of the child's own emotional, social, cognitive, moral and creative state of development, but the production of knowledge was still important. The most radical approach was the dialectical, which took its lead entirely from the children themselves: the child has to be given as much autonomy, opportunities for fantasy, movement and self-expression as possible. This approach was based on the theories of Loczy, that is, a Hungarian institution based in Budapest where ideas about children's autonomy had been developed over many years. The theory elaborates how children can develop in a carefully structured environment with the minimum of adult intervention.

The co-ordinators involved in this study had held regular training sessions with staff to try to put these ideas across and to develop them. In the nursery with the co-ordinators who were most committed to this theory, an extraordinary amount of effort had gone in to developing practice. For instance, training videos were made by staff of each other working in the nursery. They were then analysed frame by frame by the co-ordinators in staff training meetings. The result was a very remarkable nursery, where the sensitivity and responsivity to individual children, and the careful watchfulness, unobtrusive support and subtle redirection of their activities were little short of astonishing; every gesture of each child was noted, and the children's intentions were rarely misinterpreted, although the staff kept their distance and would only intervene directly if a child appeared distressed and had tried but was not able to cope.

In the other three Italian nurseries, the training had been less thorough and less carefully worked out, and in one of the nurseries it had paradoxically had a negative effect. The staff did not fully understand the implications of the theory, and took it to mean that they need not provide many resources for the children or do very much with them. These nurseries, along with the Spanish and UK nurseries, are described in detail in Chapter 5.

The co-ordinators in the Italian region were responsible for training, for developing practice and for monitoring its effectiveness. In Barcelona, the nurseries, which were organized as collectives, undertook this role for themselves. They decided as a group on their training needs, and had a budget to buy in a training consultant from a list supplied by the local authority, usually a specialist from one of the local universities. These included such themes as children's use of language; the use of aesthetic materials in the nursery; and relationships with parents.

The local authority organized quarterly meetings with the consultants to discuss the themes which had arisen and how they had been handled. In addition the professional organization Rosa Sensat, which had offered the training before LOGSE, maintained a well stocked library and ran its own courses, including a summer school, which individuals could attend if they chose.

The staff in the UK nurseries mainly had a nursery nursing qualification, known as the NNEB or BTEC. Two had a basic teaching certificate but had not practised in schools for various reasons. A few of the senior staff had acquired a basic social work qualification, known as CSS or CPQS. One had an advanced diploma in nursery nursing. One had a nursing and community work qualification. No one had a degree. Two were unqualified, but had never been offered any in-service training to address their lack of qualification.

In the UK nurseries there were no expectations that any kind of in-service or continuous training would be provided and it was not timetabled. Any post-qualifying training was expected to take place on an individual basis, and largely in the individual's own time. Although there was an assumption that post-qualification training was a personal matter, relatively few people had chosen to undertake it. Those that had taken some kind of further training or qualification had done so as a step towards seeking promotion. Although there had been some short-lived *ad hoc* efforts to introduce training, at the time of the survey there was none happening and no plans for development. There was no culture of training and development in the nurseries; sometimes the reverse. Some staff said they would welcome more training; others were resentful at the thought that they needed any further training and took it as a slur on their original qualification; yet others thought it was their employer's job to provide training in work time, and not for them to seek it elsewhere. Some staff viewed training as a kind of top-up of what they were already doing and said they welcome 'refresher training' to extend their repertoire of activities with the children and to learn new techniques, for instance, about craft activities.

Enjoying the job

Since the job varied so much from nursery to nursery, and because expectations about what the job might offer differed so much between contexts, measures of job satisfaction were not straightforward, and what would be acceptable in one country would be regarded as unacceptable in another. Staff were asked to rank different aspects of the job, and to explain what they liked best and least about it. They gave a rating of job satisfaction on a scale 1–5, and were asked to predict whether they would still be in the nursery in one and in five years' time. Not surprisingly the ratings were very high in Spain and Italy, mostly 4 or 5, and lower in the UK. Staff saw themselves as having a longer-term commitment in those countries, whereas the staff in the UK were less certain about their futures. I tried to match this information with absence rates. I asked for a record of sick leave since the level of absences is often an indication of staff satisfaction. However this was complicated by maternity leave, and long-term sick leave of staff with a chronic illness, and by the use of supply staff when there were long-term vacancies; the information proved too unreliable to use, although it was noticeable that the dysfunctional Italian nursery described in Chapter 5 had the highest rate of supply staff.

In obvious ways the staff had similar satisfactions: seeing children's progress, affection from children, rewarding comments from parents, good working relationships. But in other ways expectations and satisfactions were very different. In Italy and Spain a great deal of emphasis was put on how the nursery as a whole could review and develop its practice and think critically about it. Review and development were integral to the service. In the UK nurseries this dimension was lacking. Staff saw themselves as individuals rather than part of a group and the hierarchical organization and weak social climate of the nursery reinforced this perception. But even if the nurseries had wished to be more rigorous about their practice, their organization, and the depressed context in which they were operating made any change and development difficult to achieve.

4

The Children

The difficulties which the children show are therefore not considered a nuisance or merely a disturbance of routine but a starting point for thought and effort. They give rise to theoretical discussions and exchange of opinions. Attempts are made all the time to use and apply theoretical knowledge to solve the practical problems presented by each child
(Anna Freud, writing about the Hampstead nurseries)

Who attended the nurseries? How were the places allocated? What did the children do when they were in the nursery?

Observing the children

I observed 3-year-old children in each nursery over the period of a week. I chose to look at 3-year-olds, rather than at babies, because by 3 years it is generally accepted that children are active learners and benefit from a collective learning environment under the direction of trained staff. This is not to deny that children under 3 benefit and learn from such provision, but much of the Anglo-American education literature is ambivalent about infant learning and by default assumes that a child's educational life cannot profitably begin before 3 years. In the UK this period in a child's education is regarded as a cusp, a time of transition from the informal, intimate and casual world of home to the more structured world of education and learning. Because of the ambivalences about what age a child is ready for education, where that education should take place, and whose job it is to promote it, I was interested to see to what extent education and learning were promoted in the daycare setting of the 12 nurseries.

In the course of the week I observed the children from opening to closing time, although not necessarily consecutively. There are some advantages to not having a vocabulary in that you watch actions and gestures much more closely, although I had access to the translator for a period in each day to follow up particular

points. The observations were 'ethnographical'. I was not counting the incidences of any particular category of behaviour. I did
not want a prepared observational schedule because I did not
know what I would see. Instead I tried to note the range of behaviour displayed, and the time at which it occurred, and I tried to
understand the meaning of the behaviour to the adults involved.
If a child or adult behaved in a way which seemed unusual, for
example if an adult organized a group or spoke to a child in a
particular kind of way, then I would ask, at an appropriate
moment, 'could you tell me why you did that?' or 'why do you
think Juanita did that?'

Some of the children were also keen to draw me into their
games, and were puzzled by my poor vocabulary and pronunci-
ation. I tried to act as neutrally as possible and to avoid eye
contact so that children would lose interest in me; but some of the
children who approached me were very charming and persistent
and it would have been peculiar and clumsy to them if I had con-
tinued to ignore them, so then I did smile and show interest in
what they offered to me.

The children's background

As has I have previously pointed out, the nurseries in this study
were serving different populations of children. In Italy they were
serving prosperous and homogeneous communities. In Spain they
were serving a mixed and lively cosmopolitan mainly inner-city
community. In the UK they were serving children from bleak and
depressed public housing estates. The nurseries not only served
different populations but they also provided different levels of
service aimed at differing groups within those populations.

Italy

In the Italian nurseries 40% of the relevant age group gained a
place. The administrators regarded the service as *inadequate*
because it did not meet *all* the demand for places. So in a
commune of 60,000 a waiting list of 100 for the entire commune
was regarded as unacceptable and a sign of strain upon the
service. These publicly funded nurseries were for everyone who
wanted a place – the children of doctors, lawyers and academics,
as well as for railway clerks and factory hands. The places were
for working parents, with priority given to single parents and chil-

dren with disabilities – each child with disabilities counted for two places, although in the Italian sample of nurseries there were no children with motor disabilities. One child was deaf and one was partially sighted. There were no children who spoke a first language other than Italian. Most children attended full time; a few went home after lunch.

Almost all these children were friendly, articulate and charming, well clothed and well fed and in good health. Absentee rates were low; children were not often absent. Only one child out of the entire sample showed behaviour which was badly disordered – she was extremely aggressive and bit and kicked and terrorized other children. The staff however were extremely reluctant to categorize her behaviour as pathological. In their view she just needed more time to settle in although she had been at the nursery for several months. They had not yet sought any specialized help, nor acknowledged the need to do so.

The nurseries had regular routines. Children arrived from 7.30 a.m. or 8 and had a snack breakfast, usually altogether. There would be a period of free play, an informal jokey time, with running around and games in a hall or communal area. About 9 a.m. they would go to their group rooms, and engage in some kind of activity, engaging in projects which were supposed to enhance their sensory, motor communicative and cognitive skills. At about 10.30 or so they would then have a drink – usually freshly squeezed orange and a biscuit – and then play outside until lunchtime. They washed and prepared for lunch which was about 12.30 p.m. Lunch would be a communal affair, with two or three courses of well prepared and attractively presented food. After toileting, all children would be encouraged to have a nap or rest, and almost all the children did sleep until about 2.30 p.m. Then there would be some more activities in the rooms, inside and outside, and then tea. After tea, all the children would play together until collected by their parents.

Spain

In the Spanish nurseries 8% of the relevant age group gained a place. The places were allocated on a district basis, with the secretaries of the nurseries in the district meeting with a district official to determine the allocations. There was considerable pressure for places, waiting lists for each nursery were long, and families with quite urgent problems were sometimes unable to gain a

'There is nothing better than to go to sleep with friends'

place. The priorities were for single working parents, social need
and children with disabilities. Each child with a disability also
counted for two places, and there were slightly more disabled children in the Spanish than in the Italian nurseries, some of whom
were quite frail. The language of the nurseries was Catalan, and
this posed some problems for children who only spoke Spanish
but even more for the few Arabic-speaking children. The promotion of Catalan culture, after many years in which it was totally
suppressed, was an important feature of the nurseries, but it
meant that children were required to be bilingual and in some
cases trilingual.

A few of the children were hard to manage, and were restless
and demanding. The staff had access to specialized help, although
not as much as they would have liked. But they also had a repertoire of techniques for dealing with problematic children. For
example at rest time, the staff in one nursery had a selection of
very restful and soothing music – for instance Schumann's *kinder-
leider* – in another nursery at rest time a male member of staff sung
some folk-songs in a low key and accompanied himself on the
guitar.

The routines were very similar to the Italian nurseries. The

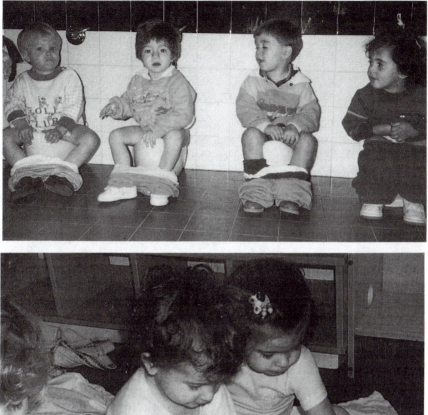

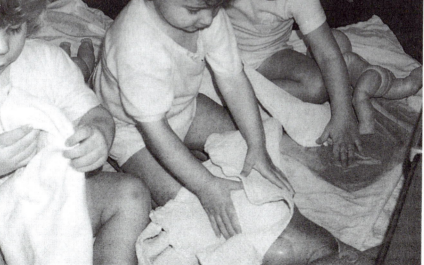

The Italian and Spanish nurseries pay attention to the physical. Whilst they are relaxed about personal privacy and nakedness, as above, they none the less consider the care of the body to be important and worth practising, as below.

groups of toddlers and 2–3-year-olds were slightly smaller, and there was not usually the space for communal play. But the days had definite and predictable rhythms which the children could anticipate and with which they were very familiar.

The UK

In the UK nurseries 1% of the relevant age group gained a place. The criterion for admission was 'children in need' – that is children who were at risk of neglect or abuse. All places were referred via social work agencies. There were long waiting lists, and complicated and cumbersome procedures for admission which served largely to protect staff against accusations of unfairness. Because of the demand for places, being a working parent was not included as a criterion for admission. The nurseries were stigmatized services, that is children were only sent to them if mothers could not manage their lives, and cope properly with their responsibilities. It was assumed that caring mothers would not work, and that nurseries were not suitable at all for children under 2. The admission of babies had been discouraged altogether. However, during the course of the research, the policy was changed. All places had been free. In order to raise money the local authority decided to sell 10 places in each nursery to working parents at a market rate. These places went mainly, but not exclusively, to babies. The nursery staff were ill-prepared for this change, and disconcerted by having more demanding paying parents, who felt no stigma and expected good services; and by having to arrange accommodation for babies. Not all these private places were taken up; in two cases the reputation of the nursery as a place where children were sent as a last resort before being placed into the care of the local authority overshadowed any demand for places and not all the private places were sold, despite the overall shortage of childcare places in the city. Apart from the private places, the places were all part time, on the principle that respite care should not detract too much from maternal obligations; and because the demand for places meant that it was regarded as better for more children to have a part-time place than fewer children to have a full-time place. Each child was given a 'package of care' according to his or her needs, as determined by the social workers, and this package varied according to circumstances and availability of places. This meant that there were no regular patterns of attendance; one child might come three mornings, another one morning and two afternoons and so on. There was no constant group of children; the group changed every morning and every afternoon.

Many of the paying places went to students from abroad, who perhaps were less aware of the history and philosophy of the nurseries. In one nursery there was a group of Arabic and west African children; in another Taiwanese and Indian children. Some of these children had a great deal of difficulty in settling because of their language, and the nursery staff just waited until the children 'calmed down'. According to one nursery nurse, 'they scream for a bit but then they get more used to our ways'. In one of the nurseries, an Arabic-speaking member of staff had been recruited, but then she was placed in a group of children who did not speak Arabic, and the Arabic children were left with an English nursery nurse 'because the parents want them to learn English and don't want them to speak their own language'.

Many of the children who attended the nurseries were depressed and distraught. In one group of 3-year-olds, for instance, not a single child could speak a sentence and some were only monosyllabic. The expectation was that the children would be poorly functioning – that was the rationale for admitting them in the first place. The situation was the reverse of the Italian nurseries. The UK staff by contrast had low expectations of what the children or their parents might achieve. The educational psychologists visited the nursery to give advice about individual children, sometimes without even seeing the children but on the basis of the records and reported comments of the staff. The nurseries used the Portage system, a systematic chart of children's progress towards various developmental milestones. Each child had a key worker who was responsible for filling in the Portage system on behalf of the child. The Portage system enabled staff to reflect on the progress of individual children, and provided a basis for discussion with parents. But it was not used in the same way in each nursery, nor did it seem to be kept regularly up to date, or used systematically except for children about whom there was a particular query, or who had a court case pending. Because of the staff shifts and holidays and the part-time attendance of the children, the key worker was often not present at the same time as the child.

The absenteeism rate of children at the nurseries was high – attendance rates were about 50–60%. An adult:child ratio of 1:8 operated for a group size of 14–16 for 3-year-olds. But the high absentee rate meant that occasionally the group was as small as five or six children with two adults in attendance. Many children were in poor health, with runny noses and coughs, and were sometimes ill-kept with dirty or smelly clothes. Even on the days when they attended many came late – children would be trickling in until about 11 a.m. or left early, after lunch. The exception were usually the foreign students' children who were dressed in smart clothes for the nursery, who nearly all had beautifully groomed hair and who were relatively punctual in attendance.

Since each child, except the children whose parents paid, had an individual 'treatment package', and since very few of these children attended full time or regularly, it was difficult to establish a sense of belonging to a group, or a daily rhythm for them. The nurseries had routines into which the children fitted when they were there – a breakfast snack at 9 a.m. or so; activities 'set up' for them; a drink of juice at around 10.30 a.m., a brief 20-minute outdoor play; then clearing up and toileting before lunch at 11.30 a.m. Then a rerun of the timetable in the afternoon. Most children were part time so there was no rest time, or indeed anywhere to rest, despite the fact that some of the children were patently tired. Many of the activities were 'closed', that is jigsaws or puzzles, or small art-and-craft type activities such as cutting out or colouring in with a predetermined outcome. There was relatively little free play, and the implicit model of learning seemed to be that children were able to learn only through the careful guidance and instruction of an adult.

In the previous chapter I noted that in the English nurseries by comparison with the collective nurseries of Italy and Spain there was little sense of a committed group of staff sharing and working towards common objectives. This fragmented and individualistic approach was mirrored with the children. Children may have been assigned to a particular task alongside other children, but it was striking how infrequently spontaneous peer-group play occurred. There was little sense of the children as a group able to influence or help each other, and in general the organizational format of the nurseries would make it difficult to achieve, even if it were considered a worthwhile objective. The overall objective was instead the surveillance and monitoring of individual children to make sure they did not come to harm. It was therefore important that the places were shared out between as many children as possible, so that each child could be routinely and regularly checked, and lapses in parental care carefully noted. This need for surveillance and monitoring took precedence over any attempt to provide a service which was carefully based on children's learning and development. It was assumed that if the service was provided that in itself would ensure that some kind of learning and development took place. The Italian educational theorist Malaguzzi (1993, p. 11), whose work is widely recognized, claims that on the contrary the group is the key concept for understanding how children learn and develop in a nursery setting:

> Interaction among children is a fundamental experience during the first years of life. Interaction is a need, a desire, a vital necessity that each child carries within. The interaction of children in small groups provides opportunities for negotiation and more frequent, dynamic communications with other children. Such negotiation and communication produces more exchange than in adult–child interaction, or at least different, and no less relevant exchanges. The group becomes self-sustaining, developing its own conversation, its own ways of communicating, acting and thinking.

These assumptions and this theoretical approach were familiar to co-ordinators and administrators in the Italian and Spanish nurseries and a *sine qua non* to most of the staff; but in so far as any theoretical assumptions underpinned the approach to children in the UK nurseries, it was that of Bowlby (1951). This approach by contrast holds that emotional security, and therefore learning, only takes place in a one-to-one adult–child relationship, and all other situations are irrelevant. The contribution of the peer group is completely disregarded.

In this chapter I have given an overview of the children who attend the nurseries, and how they spend their day. In all the nurseries in which I observed I tried to identify those children who appeared to be most vulnerable and to watch what happened to them. The nurseries exist for the children, and the most telling test of the service they offer is how they cope with the children who find it most difficult to be there. The next chapter explores the differences between the nurseries, and looks at how staff respond to children.

5

The Nurseries

[Nursery] is desirable as an escape into freedom – freedom of movement, freedom of noise, and freedom of companionship . . . the right sort of nursery school will only have so much instruction as is necessary to keep the children amused. So far from straining children, it should afford them relief from the supervision and interference which are almost unavoidable in small homes . . . children deprived of all these needs until the age of 6 are likely to be sickly, unenterprising and nervous
(Bertrand Russell, *Education and the Social Order*)

This chapter gives a short portrait of each nursery. Liane Mozere (1992), in her study of French crèches, spent several years in and out of the crèches as part of a research group trying to understand the nuances of daily practice and the dynamics of change as a new administration was being introduced. She tells the salutary story that only after the research was concluded, when she met one of the staff in a different context, that the staff member admitted that the major cause of conflict in the crèche had been about the physical chastisement of the children. There was a long-standing dispute about whether children should be smacked. The staff had deliberately and successfully hidden the issue from the investigators who had failed to identify it. An external observer working over a relatively short period of time cannot easily summarize the range of practice in a nursery or the skill and competency of staff; and as Reason (1994) has pointed out the nature of the relationship between the researchers and those being observed is more problematic than researchers commonly admit. It is with deference to the staff who work in them that these 12 nurseries are being introduced. The portraits represent an outsider's viewpoint; from the inside it may well look and feel very different. I have described the time I spent at the nurseries in the present tense to give more immediacy to the description.

Italy

In the chapter on staffing, the in-service training programme was described. All the nurseries in this sample had been part of an experiment to introduce the ideas from Loczy, the Hungarian pedagogical institute where a theoretical approach had been developed which stressed the importance of preserving and enhancing the autonomy of individual children in an institutional setting. All the nurseries had taken part in training courses in which these ideas had been discussed, and strategies had been developed for trying to put them into practice and for monitoring and evaluating how they were working. But as I show, the way in which the nurseries made sense of these ideas differed considerably.

All the Italian nurseries are purpose built and spacious with generous outdoor space. Space is a neglected concept and viewed functionally as no more than an aspect of health and safety in most of the Anglo-American literature (Weinstein and David, 1987). However in the Italian nurseries, as in parts of Germany (Burgard, 1994) space is much more; it is part of the learning context, intended not only to underpin and support daily routines but also as an aesthetic. Space, volume, texture, light and shade, colour and elegant design are viewed as part of the cultural heritage. According to one senior figure in the administration, 'aspiring architects sought to make their name by designing nurseries'. The nurseries differ from one another, and as will become apparent from the descriptions, some buildings are less successful than others from the point of view of enhancing the development of the children. But all are airy and spacious buildings, well lit by natural light and pleasantly finished. All of them have substantial gardens; it is inconceivable in the Italian spring and summer that children should remain indoors, and even in autumn and winter they wrap up and play outside when they can.

In the Italian nurseries the children's own work is not usually preserved or displayed prominently. It is difficult to raise this point, since it is an embedded practice – or non-practice. It simply does not occur to anyone to mount and pin up children's drawings or to display their models, in the way that has become almost *de rigueur* in UK nurseries. This is presumably because much more prominence is given to the group than the individual, and there is a belief that the work of some individuals should not be promoted over and above those of others. But there is also a view that although the children might have fun in making things, they

These Italian children have spent a week in the countryside and are 'celebrating the greenness'

are too young to produce anything artistic and their work simply does not merit display. When the children are slightly older, then their work as artists is taken more seriously. (I went from a bare *asilo nido* to its sister nursery school across the garden, and there children of 4 and 5 were engaged in painting elegant designs on pottery plates, inspired by a visit to the local factory. These plates were carefully preserved to be taken home.) Yet another reason for the lack of display is that far from being decorative, a room with too much display and patterning is viewed as cluttered, rather like the difference between a curtained Victorian sitting room and a minimalist room designed by Frank Lloyd Wright in which light and space are integral aspects of the ambience of the room, and other decoration is superfluous. All these Italian nurseries rely on natural finishes such as painted brick or wood, have generous and gracious proportions, and are flooded with light.

Another common feature of the Italian nurseries is the emphasis on peer culture. Corsaro and Emiliani (1992, p. 100) note that within the *asili nidi*

> a basic aspect of peer culture is children's creation and sharing of a stable set of activities or routines. Routines are important elements of peer culture because they involve activities that the

children consistently produce together; thus peer routines are communal, recurrent and predictable ... A central element of peer culture for young children is simply 'doing things together'.

This emphasis on the temperature and harmony of the group as a whole is reflected in all the nurseries, although it is manifested differently in each nursery. Since the children are age grouped, and the age range in each group is 9 months to 1 year, and the range of competency of the children is similar, then group activities are easier to organize. Malaguzzi (1993, p. 12), the renowned Italian educator, considers this grouping is essential:

In our experience, for exchanges among children to become more co-operative, the ages and developmental levels of the children in the group should not be too different. When adults initiate the choice of projects and the setting of situations, a more homogeneous age-group helps to inform the planning of decisions.

I was asked to visit and comment on a new development in one of the nurseries outside the sample, where they had experimented with extending the age range, from 1 year to 18 months. This was regarded as a daring experiment, and one which required much justification to parents and colleagues alike; a point I did not fully appreciate until I realized that it was viewed as breaching some of the implicit ideas about the importance of peer culture. This concept of the group was not at odds with the idea of 'autonomy' being developed through the promulgation of the ideas of Loczy but was another version of it; in the absence of adult intervention the children are more dependent on sorting out their relationship with their peers.

Despite their commonalties, the nurseries each had very different ethos.

Nursery 1

This is a 51-place nursery near a goods yard in a neighbourhood of well kept medium-sized to high-rise flats. The nursery has a security gate and there are concerns about condoms and cigarette butts thrown over the fence from the neighbouring 'prostitutes' alley' the other side of the garden. But there is hardly any graffiti or vandalism. Inside, the nursery is subdivided by sliding doors into three separate group rooms, with an additional soft room for boisterous play when it is impossible to go outside. There is not much display material – the building is left to speak for itself. The walls are of bare brick, there are skylights as well as suspended shades in the high-ceilinged room. The floor is made of plain light-coloured lino tiles. The room is subdivided by folding screens from the next group, and has full-length glass windows on one side, some of which are sliding windows. There is a full-length wall-mounted mirror. There is some high shelving out of the children's reach and other more accessible shelving with toys. There is a generous provision of toys, very few of which are 'closed' activities like jigsaws or matching games. There is a soft corner with a comfortable adult-sized sofa, a large rug and some cushions and a child-sized bookcase, and an additional accessible storage shelf. Each group room has its own bathroom and a side room exclusively used for naps and sleeping, and equipped with small mattresses. There is little wall display – only photos of all the children, arranged in a montage on the wall. This is used to take the register; the children sit in a group with their two nursery workers, and identify who is present and who is absent, with speculation about the reasons for those who are absent, and hopes that they will soon return to the group.

Outside there is a spacious garden, which has a separate secluded area for the babies. The garden has bushes and trees and slopes which the children enjoy using. Since the space surrounds the building, children can play outside the direct line of vision of staff.

The nursery is opened up at 7.20 by two of the staff on early shift. They put the coffee percolator on, and by 7.30 the first parent, a father, arrives with his son, followed shortly afterwards by two mothers with their children. They chat. One of the mothers talks to one of the staff about a book she has been reading with her child, *The Tiny Wolf*. One of the children goes into the kitchen to help with the coffee. A third member of staff arrives and more children. It is casual and relaxed and friendly; adults chat, exchange information, children greet each other and the staff, and play with toys and books. One child looks delighted at seeing his friends and runs to them immediately. Another pretends to make breakfast for one of the staff, and she enters into the game at once 'coffee, milk and mushrooms . . . what a combination,' she says as she pretends to eat and drink.

By 8 a.m. there are a dozen children in the room and four members of staff on duty. The children have a snack of warm milk and a biscuit or piece of bread. There are more games, a group of children play on the sofa, some other children scribble. Staff and children go in and out of the kitchen together. Each child arriving is greeted affectionately, and those that are reluctant to leave their parents get a hug or a kiss and a friendly comment, 'Mmm, you smell of fresh air'.

The smallest children go through a sliding door to the next room, but the others play. There are 20 children in the room involved in spontaneous play, but there is no fighting or aggression. A group of children drag their chairs into a line to make a train. A member of staff comes and makes train noises, and she and the children have a discussion about whether the train will go to the mountains. More children arrive, 36 so far.

This play session goes on till 9 a.m., and then the children go to their group rooms. One of the staff reads a story. The children cluster round her as she sits on the sofa. It is by now apparent that one of the boys, Carlo, is a bit of a dare devil, he wants lots of attention, and he snatches toys from other children. The staff respond by soothing and distracting him, although at one point, when he tries to pummel another child, one of the staff says sternly '*basta* – enough'. The children are encouraged to go to the toilet, but Carlo won't go. He starts crying. He is soothed again, someone strokes his hair. Then all the children play a circle singing game. After this they have some fresh orange juice. Then they line up, ready to go outside and play. This process of lining up takes about 20 minutes, since some children have to be chivvied to go to the toilet, others have to make sure they have outside shoes and coats. Those waiting wriggle about in the queue and a couple of boys break loose from it and chase each other around the room. Finally they are allowed to go out and play with bikes, spades and a generous selection of outside playthings. The children run, roam, poke the ground, grub in the bushes, ride bikes furiously and pull them over slopes, and generally occupy themselves, occasionally coming to exchange a few words with the members of staff. There are no squabbles outside. Even Carlo is busy.

At 12 it is time to go in for lunch. They stack the toys, line up again and are counted to go in. They wash for lunch, which they eat in their own rooms. The meal is brought on a trolley by the *dada*. There is a pasta dish, then cutlet and vegetables. Each member of staff, including the *dada*, is responsible for a small group of children, helping them with the food if they cannot cut it, wiping up spills and generally encouraging conversation. One child starts playing with his fork, and the others have a conversation about what you can and can't do with forks – like drinking water. This

Games with water and sand in an Italian nursery

is a temptation for Carlo who tries immediately to drink water with his fork, but is gently restrained and distracted.

After lunch they sit together whilst the register is taken, using the photo-montage. The *dada* prepares the beds, and by 1.15 all the children are lying down either asleep or nearly so.

The children sleep for approximately an hour and one half. The staff have their lunch, in two shifts, a jolly, sociable occasion. Then the children gradually wake up, the *dada* helps to clear up the beds and toilet the children, and the morning's routines are repeated with variations. The children have tea, a plate of fresh fruit. Two of the boys make horn signs at one another; the children on another table giggle and yodel. At 4.30 the parents start arriving. The children greet the parents as they come in – it is not always clear which child belongs to which parent. Some parents chat but others are in a hurry. One group of parents stays and talks in the garden for over half an hour whilst the children play around them. Carlo is inside playing with Lego. He spends 20 minutes in absorbed activity, the longest he has concentrated on anything all day, and he is irritated when his mother arrives and he wants to take the Lego with him. The member of staff skillfully diverts him: 'Well done, Carlissimo, perfect, fantastic', and puts the Lego construction on top of a shelf. He is pleased with the praise and trots off

By 5.55 the last child has been collected, and the remaining staff chat over the events of the day, and courteously answer my questions. They are used to researchers in this nursery – it is part of working life.

I have provided this lengthy and composited account of the daily routines because it illustrates a number of points. First, these routines are well known, well understood and anticipated by the children, and as Corsaro (1985) suggests, they build their own games and events around them. The routines – apart perhaps from the lining up to go inside and out – are not constricting but soothing. Even an anxious child like Carlo went to sleep without any fuss. Because they value these routines, and have spent time and effort developing them, the staff are slightly critical of parents who did not fit in with the routines.

Second, the children clearly take pleasure in one another's company. This may be partly because many of them are from single-child families and the nursery is their only opportunity to socialize with other children. They laugh and joke and play together and in this nursery it is unusual for any child to be left out of the general *bonhomie*. It is striking how little aggression there is considering this is a group of 16 robust children. The only gun game was momentary – two boys using their lunchtime bread as guns, quickly removed by the member of staff who eyed them.

Third, the staff are very alert and receptive to any overture from

Working outside in an Italian nursery

a child and respond with warmth. The staff are sensitive to each child's mood. In discussion afterwards they explain:

> It is important to let children do what they want.

> We should help them name and recognize their feelings, to let them know their good feelings so they experience the world positively.

> Unless they are happy they will not be free to experiment. This is a quiet place, we encourage serenity and tranquillity. We want them to have a happy life, and good relationships.

Although emotional responsivity is important, they are not much concerned with cognitive complexity. If children chose to elaborate and extend their tasks that is up to them, their job is to provide the climate and the materials to help them do it.

We have a discussion at lunchtime about the differences between the English nurseries and themselves. I explain that one of the preoccupations – however imperfectly realized – with the English nurseries is equal opportunities. The staff are blank, they cannot make much sense of the concept. They think that neither gender nor race warrant special treatment. Because of their emphasis on group solidarity, they have minimized the significance of any differences between children. They explain that, because of some of their recent training, they are beginning to realize that perhaps individual differences and preferences should be regarded more seriously:

> Up to now we have expected all children to eat the food we provided. Now we have decided to be more culturally sensitive. We are going to give a questionnaire out to parents, to ask them about their preferences.

> As regards racism, we are all worried but we do not know what to do. We meet very few people who can help us.

This staff group are conscious and proud of their collective identity. They go together on outings outside work, such as a trip to the cinema or for a meal, once a week, 'nothing formal, not always all of us, but together'. They were also conscious of their limitations as a group of workers. They felt they wanted more guidance: 'Not a supervisor, no one in authority, but a person to help us do the work better, a specialist to help us with individual children who have problems, to help us sort out strategies,'

Nursery 2

This nursery is sited in a pleasant residential neighbourhood of mainly detached housing. There are no problems of vandalism or graffiti. The building consists of a long wide hallway, with glass doors at each end, with the children's rooms leading off one side of the hall and the staff and utility rooms leading off the other. The hall is cavernous and echoes – it is a noisy space. The outside space leads directly from a door in each room on to wide shallow steps, and then a large grassed area. The steps are somewhat hazardous for the youngest children – I see several children stumble and fall.

The nursery, although it follows roughly the same routines as the other nurseries and is informed by the same Loczy philosophy of autonomy, appears to be dysfunctional in a number of ways.

Here cleanliness is not only a high priority but also an obsession. When the children arrive in the morning, their parents have to change them into the nursery uniform of brightly coloured tracksuits. At lunchtime the children are given bibs to put over the tracksuits. For the afternoon nap the children are changed again into pyjamas, and then when they awake, they change back into tracksuits, clean ones if there are any dirty marks. Then the parents have to change them back into outdoor clothes when they leave – a minimum of four changes of clothing! A laundrywoman is employed to look after the clothes and linen, which are washed daily.

The floor of the rooms is tiled and left as bare as possible to facilitate cleaning. The plastic tables and chairs are stacked in a corner 'to reduce the risk of accidents' and there is no other furniture save four small cushions on a shelf. There is a locked wall cupboard containing some toys and some boxes of toys on a high shelf, but no material is directly accessible to the children. Apart from a painted mural in the hall, the nursery is bare.

The floors are washed thoroughly at least twice a day. The children eat in the hall, and whilst they are having their lunch the rooms are cleaned out thoroughly with powerful disinfectant cleaning fluids. The children go back into their rooms after lunch, and the hall floor is then cleaned with the same cocktail of cleansing materials. At the end of the day the children gather in the hall, and the rooms are cleaned again. One of the cleaners is off sick, and a supply cleaner, a young man, is sent in to polish the windows. The children are sent out the room to enable him to do it. A male janitor is also sanding and varnishing some benches outside the French window at one end of the hall, and has stacked the unmended furniture just outside the window. It is not clear whom this furniture belongs to or why he is working there.

On arrival there is no system for greeting individual children or parents. Once changed into uniform by their parents in the bathroom, the children are left to make their way into the group in the hall before 9 a.m. or into the room after 9 a.m. In the room for the 3-year-olds the children have nothing at all to do. The room is quite bare and the children squabble and are fractious with each other. The staff, two of whom are supply staff, sit the children in a line for singing games. There is nothing soft to sit on except a small mat and the four cushions over which there is a great deal of squirming and pushing. One member of staff is fortunately a skilled story-teller, and the children almost cease fidgeting as they listen to her dramatic rendering of the *Three Little Pigs*. But then it is time for 'free play'. One of the staff reaches up for a basket of toys and simply tips its contents on the floor in a heap. All the toys are plastic for easy cleaning. Most of the children make a rush for the toys, grab what they can and hoard them away from other children. I see one boy protecting his toy horse, by leaning over on one side and trying to hide it in the curve of his arm, as if he is afraid that it will be noticed and snatched away. In the periods in the hall there are more toys – balls or hoops and other play-things – but the children are uncertain in claiming the toys and aggressive and quarrelsome about holding on to the toys they are using. Only outside, where there are enough toys, and interesting spaces in which to wander around, do the children become more relaxed.

Staff often look glazed or bored, or else are very rushed, for example toileting a large group of children and changing any dirty or wet clothes, before or after sleep time. The staff under stress would sometimes shout at the children: 'You can't go outside unless you are good. Be quiet. Be good.'

During the period of observations, life in the nursery is one of anxiety and stress for the children. This is exacerbated by the numbers of supply staff, and at one point one of the supply staff is left alone with a group of children none of whose names she knows, despite having been in the nursery several days. She refers to a list to try to identify the children, and some children she calls by the wrong name. I watch one 3-year-old who shows increasing signs of misery as the day wears on. He stands nearer and nearer the door and watches in anguish every time it opens. When his mother finally arrives in the afternoon he runs to her sobbing with relief.

I find it very difficult to be an observer in this nursery. I ask the staff why cleanliness is so important, and they insist that it is for 'medical reasons'; they feel they are following a prescribed pae-diatric regime. I say that I find it surprising that so few toys are available for the children, and that they are dished out in such an abrupt manner. They say that they are leaving the children 'free to fantasize' and to create their own games. Having observed little physical contact between adults and children, except in the baby room (where there were also considerably more playthings and soft spaces than for the 3-year-olds), I ask what their view is about such contact. They reply that 'you must love the children, it is most important of all'. I follow this up by asking about children who I have seen who are hard to control. In this nursery many children behave in anti-social ways – they rush around, push and snatch, pinch and pull, a sign of their unhappiness and insecurity. What do they think is the right way to deal with Andrea, for example, a boy who is particularly restive and disturbs other children? 'Ah, you mean, a child who is a leader? We let him lead'.

The staff are no different in their make-up, and the nursery no different in its general circumstances from the other Italian nurseries. The staff meet together regularly and every month bring good food to eat together after the meeting. They attend training courses on Loczy and are allowed the same amount of time for in-service training. But here for some reason the practice is unseeing. As with the nursery Mozere (1992) described there are obviously other agendas of which I do not know. The staff express satisfaction with their jobs in the questionnaires, and stress that they value 'a happy atmosphere' – which they clearly do not have – although they also indicate obliquely that there are problems with the 'administration'. It may be particular problems with absences and supply cover; there is some anger expressed about a new system of time-keeping and clocking on and off; also some bitterness about changes that are occurring at another nursery where staff are getting additional financial incentives. There may be problems over the excessive numbers of domestic staff. Whatever the circumstances, they impinge on the morale of the staff, and make it a miserable and uncomfortable place for the children to be.

Nursery 3

This nursery is on the outskirts of a small town, located in a pleasant residential area and within walking distance of a business park and the bus station. Like two of the other nurseries it is linked to a *scuola materna*, in this case as one wing of the same building. The kitchen, which produces outstandingly good food (for example freshly made pasta – cannelloni, filled with ricotta and spinach, and seasoned with nutmeg and Parmesan cheese) is shared between the two nurseries, although otherwise the staff groups are separate. The children of the *asilo* and the *scuola* do not share any rooms or outside spaces.

The *asilo* has a central hall, equipped with toys for soft play, large soft bricks, etc. The children gather there as they arrive in the morning before going to the group rooms. They play together again in the hall at the end of the day, where their parents collect them.

In this nursery the philosophy of Loczy has been most carefully worked out, the antithesis of nursery no. 2. After many sessions of in-service training over a sustained period, with staff keeping daily notes, written and with a video, about their observations and then discussing them with the co-ordinators, a method has been evolved whereby the staff are *extraordinarily* alert to each child's mood and movements. Unlike the previous nursery the attention of the staff is highly focused on the children. In the entire period of the observations it is very unusual to see a child who is being overlooked or ignored, and every nuance of behaviour seems to be followed. More remarkable still than this pitch of vigilance are the controlled responses of the staff. They do not automatically or spontaneously intervene, but make considered choices about how to react to each child in a way that maximizes the child's autonomy, and supports him or her in carrying through and developing chosen tasks.

On arrival each child is greeted, anything they have brought from home is commented on, those that are distressed are soothed and distracted, and then each child is encouraged to find his or her friends and to engage in playful tasks. Children greet each other, parents – and frequently grandparents – greet their children's friends, and arrivals and leave-takings are relaxed. Once in their rooms after 9 a.m. children are free to play.

In this nursery there is a rich and accessible range of playthings and equipment: a box of bags, hats and shoes – a red straw hat, a white beret, an airman's hat with flaps, a pair of gold high-heeled sandals, etc.; the equipment for a hairdresser's shop including a selection of shampoo bottles; a kitchen area with different kinds of real objects, bottles and glasses, funnels and sieves; and an alcove with many kinds of drawing and painting materials. Some children are absorbed in their games for long periods.

Some activities are given prominence, for example a drawing activity with magic markers, or nesting containers in the kitchen area. One morning in the dormitory the staff bring out a basket of ropes; lengths of plastic piping of different lengths and diameters, soft furry ropes, thinner shorter lengths of cord. The children, with unobtrusive help from the staff, turn the ropes, wind them round each other, blow down them, trail them, stretch them and generally put them to ingenious use, laughing and chattering. There are no requirements that children join in, except for registration time, with the photo-tree, and for lunchtime when children are expected to eat properly and with the reverence the food deserves.

The tenor of the responses by the staff is calm and soothing and considered but they are not inhibited. For instance at the end of the day when one of the boys, David, a charming friendly bubbly child, plays on the slide, slips down it and tumbles on to a soft mat roaring with laughter, then everyone in the room laughs with him, his mood is so infectious. The staff are more relaxed about the use of space than in the other nurseries, and children are able to use their dormitory room for playing in, and have more freedom to roam. Staff are watchful but do not intervene if they feel the children, even very young children, can deal with the situation by themselves.

A group of children start playing with the hinged picture window looking out on the garden. The staff member goes and stands beside them immediately, but instead of reproving or dissuading them, she says nothing until the window has been pushed back and then says softly, that it is very heavy and might be dangerous and therefore she is going to shut it carefully.

On the other hand when the staff decide that intervention is a useful strategy then it is systematically carried through. One of the children is deaf, and whichever member of staff speaks to her makes sure that she holds her gaze, and enunciates very clearly. Care is taken not to leave her out of any group conversations. One mealtime when soup is served there is some discussion with the staff member and children on the table about the properties of the soup, whether it is thick or runny, what happens when it is stirred, perhaps it is best to try it first in case it is hot. Each time the member of staff responds she makes sure the deaf child can see her and understand the conversation.

Another example of this awareness of the needs of individual children, and carefully discussed strategies of response, is the treatment of a boy who is very weepy. On and off all day, tears silently roll down his cheeks, and he stands apathetically doing nothing. Although the staff are sympathetic and informed about the circumstances which lead him to be unhappy, the strategy they have decided on is to be realistic about what they can offer him. They feel that they have to help him come to terms with his misery whereas he is using his tears as an effective ploy for attention and cuddles will reward him for this apathetic behaviour. So whilst the staff are silently supportive, a member of staff sitting next to him at lunchtime, one always nearby during the day, they are also non-interventionist, and interact with him only when he himself has initiated some activity: 'Don't worry. Don't cry. I will help you if you want to play here.'

The attention to detail in this nursery, and the extent to which the co-ordinators had theorized their approach, and worked with the staff to develop their ideas and translate them into practice, was very remarkable. No other nursery in the sample had such a coherent view about what they were doing. The staff had fully assimilated and were in almost unanimous agreement about this perspective:

> We must let the children realize that they can control things, they have the power to change themselves.

> We mustn't think of the adult as the prime mover. Adults are often acting out their own needs in dealing with children.

Effusiveness or impulsive responses towards the children are discouraged, and staff are encouraged to reflect how others see them, to co-ordinate their actions and responses towards children, to enable children to gain a sense of 'reciprocity and identity'.

The staff see themselves as being highly skilled and professional and welcome the definitive lead from the co-ordinators. Their job as staff is to offer children a secure framework, with clear rules when necessary, within which the children can fully 'become themselves' They try to 'set boundaries and help children see the significance of their actions'.

The one dissenter from this approach is one of the *dada*, an older woman who is sceptical of the theorizing, and thinks that the staff are hypocritical and pretending to agree when they do not, brushing argument 'under the carpet' But even she joins in animatedly with the group discussions, comes to the group meetings and is able to express some of her scepticism during the meeting.

It is not clear to what extent this philosophy of child autonomy was carried on into the *scuola*. The Loczy theory was developed in relation to very young children in group care, rather than for 4–5-year-olds. The chairman of the parents organization which served both the *asilo* and the *scuola* claimed that there was continuity between the two, but he sees his position as political, in that he wants to make sure that the interests of the parents are represented, that all children get places and that charges are not raised unduly. He is less concerned with the subtleties of daily organization.

This nursery is clearly exceptional. Not only do they have a coherent and child-centred philosophy but its application is also detailed and meticulous and requires a great deal of effort and commitment from the staff, who are closely supported by the co-ordinators. Some of the happiest and busiest children are at this nursery.

Nursery 4

This nursery is situated at the back of an industrial estate, and on the edge of a low-income housing estate of small semi-detached and detached houses, well kept and neat. There is no vandalism nor graffiti. The nursery is similar in design to nursery no. 2, with a large central hall with group rooms leading off at one side, and the kitchen, staffroom and other utilities at the other side. The children also wear uniforms 'it is more hygienic, more impersonal clothing so the children do not compare themselves with one another', but they do not have to change into pyjamas at rest time, or change their clothes if they become marked in any way. The noise level in this nursery is very high. The hall also echoes, and because of the almost continuous use of an industrial cleaner, as well as the washing machine, it is sometimes impossible to hear the children speak. In this nursery the children eat in their rooms, and after the meal, the cleaners come round immediately with a trolley full of cleaning materials, partly cleaning around the children whilst they are still in the room.

The staff are more interactive with the children than in nursery no 2. There still appears to be no system for greeting children on arrival or saying goodbye at night, and parents are left on their own to arrive and depart and to change their children in and out of uniforms. There is some friendly interchange, but not the warmth and communal greetings that took place between children, parents and staff in nurseries nos. 1 and 3.

When the children arrive the rooms are bare, and there are no soft furnishings. The toys are out of reach on a high shelf or in a locked cupboard. The staff talk to the children or sing a song, then in what seems to be an arbitrary gesture – perhaps in response to the children's fractiousness – as in nursery no. 2, a basket of toys is lifted down and tipped out in a heap and the children push and squabble to get hold of a toy. But the staff also provide some planned activities. In one of the morning sessions they provide dough and the children are encouraged to roll and cut the dough to make pizzas (the cleaners come in immediately after this activity to mop the floor). One of the staff has a delightful singing voice and sings to the children.

There are more cuddles and more conversations with the children, although children's bids for attention are sometimes ignored or dealt with abruptly or arbitrarily. For instance one of the staff attempts to read a story to the 18 children altogether, but sits on a stool in such a way that not all the children could see the pictures she was pointing to. The tiled floor is uncomfortable to sit on and there is a scuffle for the few cushions and for space on the mat. Three children drag chairs to sit on but in doing so obscure the view of other children, and there is more squabbling about the chairs. This leads to confrontation and tears. One child is grabbed to sit on the story-teller's knee, another is left to wander off and bawl, a third taken to the bathroom and given a dummy.

However in this group of children, there is a child – uniquely in the Italian sample – whose behaviour is very problematic. She is a large strong girl and she attacks other children frequently and snatches toys away from them. In the most extreme instances she drags a child across the room by his hair, and puts a bag over another child's head and tries to suffocate her. She is aggressive and highly attention seeking all the time and the other children are terrified of her, and draw back from any encounter with her. No other child will play with her, inside or outside, if they can possibly avoid it. I ask staff what they made of her behaviour, and am struck by their refusal to pathologize it: 'Oh, she just needs more time to settle in' (she has been there four months). They do not attempt to reason with her or segregate her; nor do they try to protect other children from her vicious pummelling or comfort them when they had been hurt or frightened. They are kind to her and patient but they have simply no strategy for dealing with her, and find it hard to acknowledge the extent of the disruption she causes, although they are very careful not to wake her up after the nap period, and she sometimes remains asleep an hour longer than the other children, to everyone's relief.

In this nursery the staff express limited criticism of the hygienic routines. One member of staff wrote in the questionnaires that the cleaning got in the way of the children; another thought the uniforms should be abolished, another commented on the unsuitability of the furnishings.

In this nursery too the collective have parties together. For one of these parties the cook made an exquisite *torta di ricotta Romagnola* (the recipe of which I carefully collected!). Like all the Italian nurseries the staff were sociable and valued their work relationships.

The *asili nido* originated as a welfare service and Law 860 established it as a custodial service for working parents, although subsequently Law 1044 fostered a broader educational and social view of the role of the nurseries. It may be that these traditions of custodial organization endured in the two nurseries where cleanliness and hygiene were so important – one of the domestic staff had been employed in the *asilo* for over 30 years; or the paediatric involvement had been of an unhelpful kind. The traditions may also have been related to employment conditions for manual workers – the cleaners, janitors and other domestics – which had guaranteed them job security even though the jobs they now did were not only unnecessary but also inappropriate. Whatever the reason, the Loczy approach appeared not to have influenced the practice or organization of these two nurseries but to have been adapted and incorporated into it and used as a rationale for continuing it.

In the other two nurseries there had been strenuous attempts to develop and extend practice, and one of the nurseries was outstanding in the way in which the staff were attentive and receptive to the needs and behaviour of the children.

Spain

In Spain the new education reform act (LOGSE) had defined education as being for children 0–16. The *escuelas infantiles* were proud to be considered part of the education system, and a prominent national politician, Marta Mata y Garriga, very closely associated with them, has attempted to define the learning and educational potential of infant education and its rightful place in the education system in a number of important public forums:

> It is precisely because of the consideration of quality and quantity in infant education, that we are obliged to reconsider the unity and diversity of education from three months to adulthood, and the problem of devising the same level of quality, with a distinctive focus for each level of education.
>
> (Mata y Garriga, 1990, p. 34)

In her view, infant education is a privilege, an opportunity to which all children should be entitled. Most staff in the nurseries shared this view of the nursery as a place where new freedoms and new opportunities to learn and behave can be offered to children: 'We don't want to get too involved in the parents life. We don't need to know their intimate lives. School is the territory of the child. Children may be rude at home, with us they make different choices' (*ibid.*).

The Ministry of Education and Science (Ministerio de Educacion y Ciencia, 1989) has provided examples of a curricular base for infant and primary schools, which, without being prescriptive, is soundly practical – examples of stories, collective and co-operative activities, drawings and music, exercise and bodily hygiene. At a city level, this emphasis on education is also prominent, with local guidelines, and again within the nurseries, there are education plans at a whole-nursery level and for each group of children.

There is a particular focus on local cultural activities – the Museum of Science and the Miro Foundation both hold special events for young children in co-operation with the authority and have visiting arrangements for the nurseries. Reproductions of well-known pictures – Goya, Picasso, Dali, Miro and Van Gogh – are displayed in the nurseries. Classical concerts are arranged so that small children and their parents can attend, and there is carefully chosen classical music in the nurseries, as well as folk-songs – but no commercialized nursery rhymes with saccharine rhythms and poor reproduction.

All children speak Catalan in the nurseries, even if their home language is Castilian Spanish. Food is perceived as an aspect of culture, and lunch is a three-course meal featuring many local Catalan dishes. Local festivals are celebrated – one nursery was part of the local literary festival of the district schools; in another some of the staff sang in a local choirs festival. Parties are frequent and lavish: 'At the end of the year we have a party for everyone on the patio. Each person brings enough food for three! The school buys the puddings and the ice-cream and champagne.'

Many of the nurseries began as local community initiatives, in the absence of state provision in the Franco years. These community nurseries attracted male workers, often teachers or graduates, who did not want to work in the formal education system (in Barcelona the proportion of male workers is 5% although in some regions of Spain it is higher). But most of the workers in these local collective nurseries had little formal training, other than that provided by the local educators' early-years network, Rosa Sensat, which ran well attended summer schools. The new parliamentary democracy and the creation of autonomous regions responsible for their own educational programmes made it possible for the city to take over and support the nurseries. The introduction of LOGSE opened up training possibilities, and in the period of 10 years, about 80% of the staff of the nurseries undertook their teacher training course at the local university on an in-service basis. The city authorities also allowed six hours of non-contact time out of a 36-hour working week, and the nurseries each had their own budget for in-service training. They could decide on topics, and use consultants from a registered list provided by the local authority to develop areas of practice. All the nurseries had staffrooms full of books and other training materials.

As in the Italian nurseries, the concept of the 'group' was an important one, and peer group relationships were encouraged and supported. There was careful attention to group size. Babies' groups were never larger than six children. Other groups might vary slightly according to the premises: eight or nine children aged 1–2; ten to twelve children aged 2–3; fourteen to sixteen children aged 3–4. Each group would have two members of staff, who alternated their shifts, overlapping from 10 a.m. to 3 p.m. The adult:child ratio therefore varied slightly during the day, but the group and its staff were always together. Each child with a disability counted as two places. There were no ancillary workers (unlike the Italian nurseries), apart from the two cooks and a part-time domestic. The staff undertook more of the domestic work for themselves. They cleaned up more, and were responsible for watering and looking after the yards and other outside spaces. One of the collective in each nursery was elected for a period of two years as a secretary. All staff were emphatic that this post, although supernumerary, carried no extra powers, status or remuneration. The secretary was responsible for most of the administration, collecting the fees, and regulating the budget, and liaising with the subdistrict over admissions.

Since many of the nurseries were existing nurseries taken over by the authority, some of the accommodation was unsatisfactory. Two of the nurseries were in accommodation that would not have been permitted in either Italy or the UK, and the Spanish health and safety standards were less rigorous than in these countries. However given the density of habitation of the city, there were few if any alternatives sites in these localities. The new nurseries that were being opened by the city were extremely well designed and spacious, some built on prime sites – for instance on the sea front – with pains-taking attention to detail. Whatever their location, the nurseries were all well equipped, with a wider and more stimulating range of learning activities than any of the Italian nurseries.

Playing and working in the courtyard of a Spanish nursery

Nursery 5

This nursery is in an inner-city working-class area. It is situated
on the top two floors of an apartment block, and the roof space
serves as the outside play area. There are two staircases that link
the floors, one a steep spiral staircase originally for servants. The
kitchen is in the centre of the lower floor, and two parts of the
lower floor of the nursery are traversed by going through the
kitchen. The kitchen has a bar top to separate the cooking area
from the through corridor. Children ride their bikes through the
kitchen corridor in the period after lunch and chat with the cooks.

The roof space is well equipped with sand and water, ropes for
swinging, and other materials such as chalks for pavement
drawing, and it is bright with flowers in pots, but it is a constricted
space and the wire netting which surrounds it is old. Parts of the
roof space are being renovated during my visit, so the space the
children have is less than what is usually available, and I worry
about the numbers of highly active children in such a small space.

I find the nursery hazardous, and inquire about accident rates.
The staff assure me that accidents are unusual (although I do see
one child graze his cheek – he does not cry but thinks that the
blood is an interesting phenomenon and points it out to me –
'Look, blood!' in an excited voice.) The staff argue that the way
to deal with the difficulties of the accommodation is not to shield
children from them, but accustom them to dealing with them, by
giving clear instructions and helping them to understand the
dangers. I watch a worker carefully discussing the effects of
opening a door to a child on a bike, and they try out several ways
of reaching the door and opening and shutting it, before the
worker is satisfied that the child has grasped that he might endanger himself or others if he is not careful. Similarly very young children, barely walking, are helped up and down the stairs, with the
workers coaxing them and encouraging them.

This nursery opened in 1968, and had been taken into the
authority in 1983. Like nursery no. 3, its aims and objectives are
clearly articulated and systematically put into practice. The aims
of the nursery, formulated and revised over time, are to

- promote conviviality between children;
- give all children an opportunity to play and to use the materials
  provided;
- use the active intervention of the teacher to promote interaction
  and learning to the benefit of all children;

- offer both male and female role models to children; and
- work positively with families, in such a way as to assure the mother that she was not exclusively responsible for the care of her child.

The values of the nursery are defined as 'tolerance, solidarity, co-operation, respect for diversity, rebuttal of authoritarianism, and respect for the rights of young children.' These aims and values are spelt out in terms of the curriculum and organization of the nursery, so that the activities which take place refer directly to the underpinning aims.

This nursery is striking in its expectation that children are responsible learners, capable of being self-controlled and self-reliant, and of being aware of the needs of others and of the group. This may have originated from the requirements of the building, but it is undoubtedly part of the ethos of the nursery. Children are spoken to seriously, as fellows. Each child is greeted when he or she arrives, with a kiss if asked for. On the other hand if children are considered to be behaving inappropriately they are ignored. For instance one child who weeps copiously and melo-dramatically is ignored until he stops, and then the worker joins in a game with him to which he responds eagerly. A partially sighted boy who removes his eyepatch is also ignored; his eye-patch is handed back to him later without comment, and he puts it back on.

Even the babies are encouraged to taste new foods and put their bibs away in their bags after eating. One child who appears to have finished and toddles away from the table comes back and asks for more food. She is refused – 'finished is finished,' says the worker gently. Older children are encouraged to help with younger children, and the babies' group room has been deliber-ately placed next door to the oldest group of 3-year-olds, and there is a carefully prepared interlude in which one of the babies joins with a group of 3-year-olds at their table; and another when two 3-year-olds are allowed to go to help in the baby room.

The oldest group are exceptional in the amount of co-operative challenging and sustained play they engage in. There is a wide and stimulating range of activities, including theatre and pup-petry, many kinds of construction toys, modelling materials, and files containing children's photos and generous provision of books. There are play areas that are raised and separated from adult scrutiny, a well equipped kitchen area and sink with some real fresh vegetables, and a cockpit reached by a ladder. There are two tanks with small turtles whose feeding and care are frequently commented on. The children have more or less complete freedom to choose their activity from breakfast until about 10.45, but it is assumed that the children are responsible for getting out, continuing with and thoroughly clearing up the activity. Any activity, once begun, has to be properly completed.

The result of this approach seems to be that children play with sustained concentration. During the week I spend in the nursery no child leaves an activity uncompleted, and there is simply no aimless play – a situation which I have never seen anywhere else in many years of nursery visits. Some games or activities involve complex interactions with several children, e.g. a puppet play about the three little pigs, and lasts for an hour or more. The children using construction toys to build very elaborate designs; the children in the kitchen chop, pour and measure. The nursery workers act as classroom consultants – for instance helping the children check the sequence of the play against the text in the book. They move from group to group, from child to child, checking that there are no obvious difficulties, listening to plans and commentaries, and giving children advice on how to extend an activity, making sure that they are carrying through their intentions and do not get diverted, and making sure clearing-up is thorough – the kitchen for example has to be immaculate!

The group times when children sat in a circle are entertaining as well as obligatory. For instance the nursery worker uses the device of a large hand-held puppet to get the children talking and joking and thinking. The puppet holds something behind his back and says: 'What have I got behind my back, its not something to eat, its not a plant, its not an animal, what is it?' The children make guesses, with the puppet teasing them, and then magically an umbrella pops up from inside the nursery worker's T-shirt.

This is very skilled interactive teaching, drawing on the sustained organization and ethos within the nursery. The staff are vigilant, proactive, but not interfering, and the price of their vigilance is exhaustion at the end of the day. They work themselves very hard. Children who have been in the nursery full time for two or three years understand clearly how it works and what is expected of them and are busy and thoughtful.

There were a few children however who find it difficult to fit in. At the time of my visit two children in the nursery have disabilities, one moderate, one severe (the latter not in the 3-year-old group, although the 3-year-olds play with her at carefully arranged times.) A third very ill child had just died. These children are carefully attended to, and have support from physiotherapists and educational psychologists, some of it provided at the nursery itself.

More problematic are Arabic-speaking children from north Africa in a younger age group, for whom the language, the cultural expectations and the nursery routines appear puzzling. One small girl, at afternoon rest time, thrashes about on her mattress as if she has a demon within her, and it takes all the nursery worker's patience and skill to calm and settle her. Other Arabic-speaking boys shout to each other in Arabic on the roof-top playground and play rough games which sometimes endanger other children. In principle, as their aims suggested, the nursery workers respect diversity, but in the case of the Arab children, their careful teaching strategies and promotion of Catalan culture are not sufficient. The Arab mothers come to the nursery and chat freely with each other and with the staff when they bring and collect their children, so given the attention to detail in the nursery, and the goodwill of the parents, perhaps it is a matter of time for these issues to be resolved.

Nursery 6

This nursery is situated in a pleasantly converted house in a leafy suburban area. The nursery, like the others, had started off as a community collective, and had served a mainly middle-class catchment of professionals – doctors, lecturers and small-businesspeople. The catchment had changed as the municipality took over, and there are now a greater proportion of children who, in the view of some members of staff, are less well brought up, and who present more problems.

This nursery too is well equipped, and has an imaginative range of materials and activities for the children, and a lovely shaded courtyard as an outside play area. The cooks, as in all the nurseries, are a lynch-pin of the organization, and provide good food at a low cost, and sit in on the staff meetings and contribute to the organization.

In this nursery however it is much harder to be an observer, and my presence as an observer is discomforting to some of the staff, a situation exacerbated by the fact that two of the members of staff are ill, and there is a problem about finding experienced

supply staff. There does not appear to be the systematic co-operation and planning between staff that I saw at the first nursery,
and there seems to be some tension about styles of interaction
with the children, one worker very firm with the children, another
taking a more liberal approach. The group of children I am watch-
ing are slightly more disruptive, and less self-reliant than in the
first nursery, and the staff do more for them, serve them with food,
tidy up after them, help them dress, all of which the children were
able to do for themselves in the first nursery.

The children's behaviour in the classroom is also more aimless,
and less focused, with flitting from activity to activity, and staff
failing to observe or follow up individual children. For instance I
watch children who have started off playing with cars in a garage
get bored, stuff the cars in a dolls house, run off and play in the
kitchen area, then leave after a few minutes to flit through some
books. Scarves which have been used for a dancing lesson are
dropped and trampled on.

But all this is relative. The first nursery is very exceptional and
the second nursery is burdened with staff absences at the time of
my observation. It is still a good place for children to come, where
there is freedom to play with the generous and imaginative materials provided, and the staff are long-serving and dedicated. A
child with Down's syndrome is treated by the staff and by the
other children in a supportive way – he wandered between group
rooms as the children were settling in the morning and adults and
children greeted him warmly, as he clutched a plastic bottle half
full of beads. On a subsequent visit I come back for a surprise
birthday party for a member of staff, which is a terrific affair in
the local community; a table laden with wonderful food, baked
meats, sauces, tortillas and salads prepared by the cooks, lavish
wines, and a celebration, amongst other things, of the pride experienced by the woman whose birthday it was at having had the
opportunity to study and gain a professional qualification after a
lifetime of hard work. This kind of conviviality cannot exist in a
vacuum – it is a reflection of warm relationships and shared work
over a long period of time.

Nursery 7

Like the first nursery, these premises are unsatisfactory. The
nursery is in a small dilapidated street of old houses, but the street
is in an area which is rapidly being redeveloped, and all around

The cooks in a Spanish nursery. Despite the poor working conditions the cooks produced delicious regional dishes using local produce

are new elegant high-rise flats and smart offices. The building itself is a small cramped house with unsatisfactory toilets, and the kitchen and one of the group rooms are in an out-house across a courtyard. The kitchen, where meals are prepared and the staff eat, seems precariously equipped; not enough working surfaces, erratic electricity and spasmodic water pressure, and is due for urgent renovation. There is also a roof garden reached by a spiral staircase. The courtyard is walled, with many pots of flowers attached to the walls, and a shady tree with a seat in the middle. The ground is sandy earth which is trailed into the rooms by the children. The staff acknowledge the difficulties of working in the house, but insist it is preferable to a new and more sanitized place.

In this nursery the pleasure the staff take in one another's company, and in the children, is palpable. There seems to be an implicit view amongst most staff that of all the places in which one could choose to spend one's time this is it. There is a kind of *joie de vivre* which expresses itself not only in the staff spending much more time in the nursery than they are contracted to do, staying on to help on each other's shifts, but also with much physical affection and laughter. I watch a young member of staff and the older cleaner stroll up and down the courtyard, their arms around one another, deep in conversation. One member of staff in particular gives enthusiastic kisses to every child on arrival, and to some of the parents and their accompanying children, as well as to other staff. ('handsome' she says to a small boy, and gives him a wet kiss, then kisses his older sister who is on her way to school; 'you please me' she says to another child as she bestows a kiss).

As an English observer for whom such physical expression of mood is unusual, I worry about her extravagant kissing, but no one else seemed to consider it intrusive. The children cluster around her like chickens round a mother hen, such is her warmth and glow. For instance, Marco, involved in a game with cars at the other end of the room, points to the traffic queue he has made line up at the lights; she shouts her delighted approval from the other end of the room and he runs to her for a kiss, before going back to his traffic-control post. Two children come into the room crying. The member of staff sits them down to talk about it, makes soothing remarks, and then kisses one of the children on the back of the neck and tells him to be careful. He squirms with pleasure.

Although this particular member of staff is extravagant with her kisses, almost everyone shows physical affection uninhibitedly. A toddler strays into the kitchen, the cook picks him up, kisses him and passes him outside, where he is passed around amongst several staff and children, all of whom also kiss him. The children often solve arguments and seal their peace with hugs and kisses, boys as well as girls, sometimes at the direction of the staff, sometimes spontaneously.

The nursery was known as the most anarchic of the collectives which the city adopted, with the children free to wonder from group to group, and to choose the members of staff with whom they related. Over the years this approach has been modified, and the children are now age grouped with their pairs of staff, as in the other nurseries. But there is still more interchange between the groups than is usual. The male member of staff responsible for the babies (who plays Bach piano music to them from a tape) brings them into the courtyard, in a fenced-off area, but with opportunities to interact with other children. Groups sometimes eat their tea outside at a big table; the oldest group are free to play inside or outside their room. Staff create puddles in the yard with the hose, and fill buckets of water. Children from several groups are allowed to play together: there seem to be a lot of toddlers in the yard mixed up with older children – there is amiable digging, scrabbling and pouring; they make sandpies. The worker tastes the sandpies with extravagant gestures, blowing and sniffing at the pretend food, 'how good, how delicious'. Then without any obvious instructions the children sort themselves out into their groups again, and one group goes inside.

In this nursery, as with all the others, there is the same emphasis on learning, creative activity and cultural events. As an observer I can hardly believe my ears when a member of staff puts on a Mozart chorale on the tape and asks the children what it is. The children shout the *'The Magic Flute'* (they had heard Papageno's song earlier in the morning) but she says seriously to these 3-year-olds 'it is by Mozart, he wrote a lot of music, but this is something else to listen to'. She points out how the sounds differ from the earlier piece: 'The mens voices are deeper.' The children

The attention to design and cultural detail in a Spanish nursery. This was part of a project about dragons and devils

listen attentively. A little later a group of children are discussing the colours used in a painting by Miro – lots of dark blues, and they are encouraged to reproduce the shades of blue in their own paintings. There is a file of Miro paintings for them to consult. The blues the children produce are then compared with each other; they discriminate easily between the shades of blue.

The staff discuss, explain and shower the children with praise and affection. Since a majority of children who attend the nursery are the only children in their families, the nursery includes as part of its written aims to 'offer security, stability, affection, an opportunity to know and to share good and bad times with one another'. Love and friendship is a major discourse in this nursery:

If you are caring to the children they will be caring to each other.

If the adults are happy, so are the children.

Its a good feeling to be working here.

Our cooks are very good, we cherish them.

There are indeed many instances of affection and caring amongst the children. Two boys have a mock boxing match, it veers on being rough, then they draw back and walk off hand in hand. A child desperately wants to use a magic marker – the girl using it sees this and smilingly hands it over. One child falls over, and another comes to her aid, hauls her up and dusts her down. Older children look after and watch out for little ones.

At the same time there is also a detailed educational plan, for the nursery as a whole and for each group of children, which has been worked on over many years, and which is reviewed with the training consultant in the training sessions. One manifestation of the attention to detail is the respect for possessions. Toys are carefully put away. For instance I watch one tear-away little boy, at the request of the member of staff, pains-takingly pick up dozens of plastic soldiers from the sand, after the box two other younger children were playing with was knocked over (for which of course he is rewarded with a kiss). Whilst the level of attainment in this nursery is not as exceptional as in the first nursery, and the atmosphere is more relaxed and happy-go-lucky, this too is a nursery which, in the words of the politician, it is a privilege for children to attend.

Nursery 8

The fourth nursery is in a rougher working-class district, but newly housed in beautifully designed premises built inside the shell of a row of terraced houses, sandwiched between a little public park and an OAPs club (which is almost riotous in the afternoons, with lively dancing, drinking and laughter). There is graffiti on the outside walls, and the security system of the nursery uses a video-camera of the outside door with a screen and answer phone in each group room, which is checked before anyone gains admittance.

The nursery is on two storeys, with wide shallow inside and outside staircases, and a carefully constructed courtyard with a fountain under which the children can play. The large kitchen is designed as the hub of the nursery. It is extremely well equipped, and contains a huge table at one end where children come for their breakfast and for occasional discussions, and where staff eat their lunch. There is also a generous and well equipped staffroom.

Like all the other Spanish nurseries this is very well equipped, with a plentiful range of activities indoors and outside, and spaces exclusively for the children's use. For the oldest group this is a kind of ark at ceiling level reached by a small staircase. The toilet area is an unsecluded open alcove in the room; the children have no inhibitions about its use.

Despite the spacious elegant premises, the staff in this nursery are more ill at ease than in the other nurseries. Like the other nurseries it had been independently run, and had been taken over by the city when it was rehoused, but this has happened recently, and not all the staff were happy with the change-over. The staff questionnaire indicates that there are tensions amongst the staff about ways of working. The staff work separately from each other, closed off in their own rooms and the age groups of children do not mix as in the other nurseries.

In the group of oldest children, the male teacher has a didactic style of teaching. He imparts knowledge which he expects the children to absorb. The word he uses continually is 'venga, venga' (come here, come here). He addresses the children frequently with vocatives 'wait, wait; listen listen; quiet, quiet'. He has long group sessions in which he explains the organization of the day, and during which the children invariably fidget. For instance it is a hot day and the children are being allowed to play in the fountain. The preparations for this take nearly an hour. The children must use the toilet, take off their clothes, change their shoes into plastic sandals, go down the stairs and then they are rubbed with suncream. Finally, for just over five minutes the children are allowed to run joyfully under the spray of water. Then they have to lie face down on their towels in the sun for 10 minutes to dry off, then hurry back to get ready for lunch.

Other activities are also dominated by this organization and processing of the children to make sure everyone takes part in each activity. There is a session of sponge and stencil painting, but each child has to produce a finished product to take home. Only two or three children can paint at a time, so there is a queue of children waiting to paint, and children who have finished are wandering aimlessly in the room and squabbling. The picture has to be completed in a certain way, and the teacher gives a string of instructions: 'Come on, come on, no this way, blue, no this is blue, press, no, wait wait, watch me watch me, no, use all of the space, all of it, Arancia, *por favor.*' There is an interval whilst the teacher realizes he has not prepared enough paper and has to get some more. At the end of this activity each child has a picture to take home, but at some social cost.

The other member of staff with the group, a woman teacher, has a more gentle approach but is constrained from making her views known. I attend a parents evening, where both staff jointly interview a somewhat distraught single mother, who wants to explain her concerns about her child and her own reactions to the child's behaviour. In the 20-minute interview I count thirty-five utterances by the male teacher, and six by the woman teacher, five of which were ignored or cut short by her colleague.

The intimate physical handling of the children by a man – preparing them for their nude play in the fountain, creaming their bodies vigorously with suntan oil, towelling them down and in settling them to sleep, when one fidgety girl was hauled on to his lap and held there firmly – is another aspect which as an English observer I find surprising. Such is the concern for child abuse that men touching children in this way would not be allowed in an English nursery. But when I raise this with administrators, it is regarded as unproblematic, and as an Anglo-American obsession. Within the staff group it was also unproblematic, as is the issue of male dominance:

Nudity is more of an issue now I suppose. There was a time when we were all nude with the children, when we were hippies.

Men and women are different, there is nothing in that. You expect men to be a bit rougher.

Here the staff discourse is more discontented. Some of the staff are critical of those in other nurseries who said they were enthusiastic about their job: 'People lie about how much they like it ... they show off about how much they like it, they even run courses, they think they know everything.' Whilst they agree that working for the city was better than being in the private sector several of them are dissatisfied:

I would leave tomorrow if I could, you get tired after being in the same job.

All these changes we have been through are emotionally draining.

There is not enough money, there has been no pay rise after all our training.

It's much more difficult if you don't have a husband to support you.'

However the parents evening ended in a party, for which the cook and her assistant had been preparing most of the day – trays of tortillas, cakes and wine. The photograph albums in the staffroom provided a record of many such parties. The life of the nursery in Spain, as in Italy has celebratory and convivial aspects, whatever the grumbles of staff.

The UK

As I indicated in the introductory chapters, although the staff groups in the nurseries were similar in make-up in each country, and in each nursery I was observing 3-year-olds, there the resemblance ended. Whereas the Italian and Spanish nurseries were regarded by the local administration and by the staff as a highly positive service to working parents and their children, and in the nurseries I observed, reflected a fairly cohesive society, in the UK they were mainly a welfare and surveillance service for children from very distraught families and situated in areas where social cohesion had largely broken down. All the nurseries had suffered vandalism and break-ins, and one of them was surrounded with barbed wire and had an armed night-time security guard. The neighbouring school had been burnt down, and had been rebuilt as a fortified building with high walls and barred windows; and female staff were escorted in and out of the building.

Families and their children were treated as social work clients for whom individual 'care plans' had to be made. Only in one of the nurseries was there any sense of a peer group, or of the pleasure children might gain from each other's company. In fact because of the pressure on places from social workers concerned about their clients, one place might be shared between several children, but because of the preoccupation with individuals, the portioning of time was done without any regard for the need to maintain a consistent group of children. So distressed children who attended two or three times a week were likely on each attendance to be in a different group of children.

The ratios were also organized differently. The concept of the group has little meaning, and there are no requirements for group size. Because there has been little discourse or dialogue about what collective provision might offer children other than respite care, the ratios are devised in such a way as to mimic mother–child relationships as closely as possible. The regulations require ratios of 1:3 for children under 1; 1:5 for children aged 2–3; and 1:8 for children 3–5 at all times. There is a 'key worker' system, but because there are fluctuating groups, and complicated staff shifts which also had to take account of holiday times, and since the nurseries were open all year, the key worker system did not work in practice – it merely meant that one worker was responsible for writing up case notes, but children might experience several different workers in the course of a day or a week. Since children did not attend for full regular days, there was also little consideration for the variations in the pace or rhythm of the day as experienced by children, and how staffing might accommodate to this.

Each of the nurseries also had two supernumerary members of staff, the officer in charge and the deputy officer in charge, although the administrative burden was less than in the Spanish nurseries.

All the nurseries interpreted the ratios generously, and staffed for a potential 100% full-day attendance; but in fact because of the complicated referral system involving social work assessment; because of the disorganization of the families whose children were admitted; because children attended for less than a full day, there was also a low attendance rate, and a high vacancy rate. Nurseries were almost empty after 3 or 4 p.m. although they were technically open until 6 p.m., and for much of the rest of the time they were operating at a 60% attendance level. By comparison with Italian and Spanish nurseries, these nurseries were grossly overstaffed. However the staff saw themselves as overstretched and under pressure, and indeed there was a dispute about how attendance figures were calculated, some nurseries including vacant part-places, others refusing to do so, some making allowances for holiday periods, etc.

There was also an overwhelming preoccupation with health and safety in the UK nurseries. Since a number of children had been offered places because of suspected child abuse, their safety and monitoring were of paramount concern. Health and safety regulations were concrete and in a situation where so much else of the daily routines was uncertain, their observation provided a definable measure of quality – staff were doing their job properly by being health and safety conscious. Whereas the Spanish nurseries had been relaxed about health and safety, and administrators considered even unsafe premises could be used by competent staff, the UK nurseries were by contrast almost hysterical about safety. One nursery had mounted a display in the vestibule where parents gathered entitled 'How safe is your child?' It listed all the safety hazards that threatened children, which were most dangerous to which age child and what precautions and restrictions were necessary to avoid any risks. This display had won a prize in a competition organized by a local trust. The staff meeting I attended in this nursery was used to discuss all the hazards that the nursery might present to children. One hazard identified was a small clump of nettles in a corner of the garden, and the officer in charge agreed to write a memo to the council about it, to make sure the nettles were cut down; in the mean time the children should be forbidden this corner of the garden – an absurd escalation of a very simple problem! A proposal to visit the local city farm was also turned down on the grounds that the animals presented too many hazards to the children. In another nursery every bump and knock was recorded in the accident book; a child wriggled and fell off his chair and was immediately rushed to the medical room and examined, and the accident noted – a precaution that was regarded as absolutely necessary for a child who had been abused.

Outside space was used very cautiously because of the dangers it presented – and because of vandalism – and indeed the outside space at one nursery, not included in the sample, had been closed altogether for 18 months because the outside slope had been regarded as too dangerous. Physical affection was rare. Children were hardly ever kissed or cuddled, or even touched except to be cleaned up.

The nurseries were purpose built, but the space requirements were meagre compared with the spacious Italian nurseries; the rooms were less than half the size, and there were no spare rooms nor any central space. Children were not expected to sleep during the day, and had no space or soft areas in which they might do so. They were not usually allowed near the kitchens, which were strictly functional and in no case contained eating or preparation space for children or staff other than the cook. The play rooms were small and confined, and there were no alcoves or spaces where children might hide from adult eyes. The rooms, as well as being wall papered and curtained, were cluttered with decorations, every available space being used with a display but these were frequently of Walt Disney cartoon figures, or colouring-in or glued pictures made to a standard pattern. Sometimes mobiles were pinned to the ceiling and dangled just above the heads of the staff. There was neither the uncluttered elegance of the Italian nurseries, nor the cultural images of the Spanish nurseries. In so far as there was any coherent visual rationale, it was that of a sentimentalized prettiness, a determination to shut out the bleak outside world and create a world of innocent and passive childhood within.

Outside play spaces were vandalized, poorly maintained and on the whole infrequently used, even although the period of investigation was in the summer months. No nursery grew flowers.

The staffrooms were bare empty places, and none of them contained any reference books or teaching aides for staff to consult. The staff hierarchies are powerful. In two of the nurseries if the officer in charge visits the room, it is like the pope descending! The staff become silent and watch what they say and do for fear of reprimand (for similar reasons, and for fear of being singled out, some of the staff in one nursery would not fill in the staff questionnaire). There is a team leader system in the rooms, so that the hierarchical relationships are frequently played out again in lesser form. Some of the staff feel themselves to be very junior indeed. In this context the activities of the union are important as a source of pro-

tection for the workers, and there were several outstanding grievances in the nursery service at the time of my visit.

There were no written guidelines about activities in the nurseries provided by the administration or by the officers in charge
but in each nursery I asked if I could be provided with a summary
of the aims and objectives of the activities which went on in the
nursery. These were very basic. The equipment between nurseries
varied but there was a preponderance of small plastic toys: Fisher
Price Farms, Duplo Farm, Play People, Little Tikes, My Little Pony,
Popoids, Octons, Transport Cutters, etc.; toys known by their com-
mercial name rather than by their function. The planned curriculum consisted of a listed rotation of these toys, so that no toy was
used more than once or twice in a week.

Nursery 9

This nursery is sited in a grim area, where many people are unemployed, and many of the houses have been vandalized or fired. It
is situated above a health clinic, and in premises rented from the
health authority although there seems to be little contact with the
clinic. It is a 50-place nursery, although an unascertainable number
of places are vacant: probably between 10 and 12. I cannot get a
direct answer to my question about vacancies. I think this is not
subterfuge; they simply do not have criteria for counting and
adding up all these part-time places.

There is access to an outside play area, but it is a rough over-
grown grass slope, with two stringy bushes and a broken seat. It
is used once for 20 minutes during the period of observations.
Instead there is a short plastic slide within the room, which is the
only opportunity offered to the children for exercise. They rarely
use it although it takes up so much space.

All the materials in the room are carefully stored and labelled
(although some of the labels are misspelt) and the staff make sure
that everything is put back in its proper place after use.

This nursery is overstaffed, again a problem about the calcula-
tions which are adopted. Since the officer in charge denies that
this is the case, I keep records throughout the period of observation of the numbers of adults and children. In the room in which
I am observing at 8.40 a.m. there are three staff and four children;
at 9 a.m. six staff and ten children; at 9.10 a.m. seven staff and
twelve children. One more child arrives much later in the
morning. Lunch is between 11.30 and 11.45, then some children

leave and others arrive. At 12.20 there are six staff and ten children, by 12.30 p.m. there are fifteen children. Staff take their lunch breaks, and during this period until about 2 p.m. there are four staff to fifteen children. By 3.30 most of the children have left; but there are four staff and six children who remain. The officer in charge and the deputy are supernumary and are not counted in these ratios. I am informed that two members of staff are absent and they are short staffed today; moreover some of the staff are trainees and cannot be counted in the ratios.

When I ask if there are any educational aims for the nursery, the officer in charge writes out the following in longhand for my benefit. It does not exist as a document to be consulted but only as a plan in her head:

> Our nursery programme is planned by the staff team within each group room with age appropriate activities. Each room has a furniture plan – carpet area, home corner, climbing apparatus, sand, water, messy table and construction tables. The teams have to hand their own guide to the yearly programme of planned activities and guidelines to the methodology of daily routine. This is a useful tool for new staff members and students for reference . . . Our aim is to provide a healthy happy educative environment for the developing child.

When I inquired in the rooms about the team guide, I was shown the usual rota of toys pinned to the back of a cupboard.

The numbers of staff mean that the children are closely supervised and regulated the whole time, and also that there is also continuous clearing up and tidying. For instance two children attempting to do a jigsaw barely have time to move the pieces before a staff member says 'look this goes here, doesn't it'. Two staff sit with a group of children using Lego, helping them to make identical cameras with identical colours. A child absorbed in painting, and tracing his brush over the border of the paper and easel is told 'you must keep on the paper, you put your brush here like this. Tell me which colours you are going to use'. The child then gives up the painting as soon as the member of staff has moved away. Another child, giving a tiny plastic tyrannosaurus dinosaur a ride in a car is told 'tyrannosauruses don't ride in cars, do they?' He has to take the dinosaur out, and is watched whilst he puts the car away in the proper tray. Only for the very brief period outside are the children allowed any undirected play or unrestricted movement or unsupervised activity.

The group times are didactic. Children are required to identify shapes or colours or sizes: 'Find me the red circle'. 'Which square is big and which is little?' The children must discriminate between these shapes but the staff fail to give an accompanying explanation about the properties of the shapes, and it becomes a guessing game, although the staff get cross at the inaccuracy of some of the answers and repeat their words: 'This is a large purple square not a pink circle.' The children are read stories and asked closed questions about them: 'Why do we need water?' 'We need it to water the plants, don't we?' Banal nursery rhymes are sung tonelessly to a squeaky tape on the tape-recorder, and children enact various familiar lines – for instance putting their hands together and their head on their hands to symbolize sleep; or a finger on the lips for 'shh!' – a very different musical experience from *The Magic Flute* and the men's chorale in the Spanish nursery.

The 3-year-old children were addressed by their room leader in highly articulated slowly delivered sentences, often using the first person plural: 'We don't do that in here, do we?'

The children are gathered together before dinner for a story, whilst other members of staff clear up or set the tables, or help the children wash ready for lunch. When they take children into the toilet, the staff wear disposable plastic gloves and aprons, because of the risk of infection. Then one by one each child is required to find a chair with his or her name on it and sit down quietly. Staff eat with the children at the tables – there is only one course but plentiful helpings.

The food is well prepared, but the cook is apologetic about her contribution. She has been there for many years and she likes the children. She used to come into the rooms, but because of fears about abuse, the officer in charge has interpreted the regulations to insist that only the staff directly responsible for childcare are allowed in the rooms with them. The staff sit with the children. The team leader is stern about manners. When a child wriggles from his chair and slips on to the floor, he is told to stay there. He protests that it is dirty. 'You get what you deserve,' says the worker sharply.

Instructions for routines such as lunchtime are usually clear, and children are thanked politely for carrying them out, or admonished if they fail to obey. In this nursery there are clear instructions for behaviour (although not for learning activities), and very little ambiguity. The children, and for that matter the staff, are always told what is expected of them. The routines are predictable and carried out with unvarying regularity. Children are never allowed to be aimless; someone is always at hand to direct them. This is a very highly structured situation, and for children as disorganized as some of the children attending, this routine offers a degree of security.

The poverty and disorganization of the families is considerable. One ragged child arrives with odd shoes, neither of which fit, and one of the members of staff goes off to find a matching fitting pair from the collection of jumble in the deputy OIC's room (her job during the week I am here appears to be to collect the jumble for a sale at the end of the week). Children on the abuse register are carefully checked for marks and bruises each day. For children whose life is chaotic, this nursery is a safe and predictable but highly restricted environment. The officer in charge tells me with maternal fondness that some of the children who now come are the sons and daughters of parents who themselves attended the nursery – a somewhat double-edged source of pride since the nursery is intended to help families cope sufficiently so that they no longer need to use the nursery, and this continuity of attendance is also a mark of failure.

Nursery 10

The nursery is in a less deprived working-class area than the previous area. The building is free-standing in its own grounds, but it is very cramped. There are four group rooms, all small and crowded, uncomfortable and ugly. Apart from the baby room, there is nowhere comfortable for children to sit even when they have a story or a taped nursery rhyme.

The children come from distressed backgrounds in all the nurseries, but in this nursery there seems to be a particular concentration of children with difficulties. In the group of 3-year-olds on one morning there is not a single child who can speak a sentence, and several are monosyllabic. One child shows me an animal book but cannot say the names of the animals other than the first consonant – he makes the motions, trying to bark like a dog, or miaow like a cat. Some of the children are very dirty. One child has greasy tangled matted hair, and the nursery worker patiently brushes it smooth; another child is very raggedly dressed and he, his older brother and his mother smell badly. Another child does not react at all to any other child or adult in the room, but in a very ungainly manner barges from table to table

– although outside I notice his social skills are better; he can communicate to the extent of being able to share and take turns on a bike and cart with another child.

In this nursery the OIC prides herself on her team involvement – although this is not a perception shared by her team, some of whom complain that she is rarely in the rooms and does not fully appreciate the pressures the staff experience. When I ask for a statement of aims and objectives, the OIC writes in handwriting again:

> Planning within the nursery involves the full staff team and management staff team. This involves discussion at the following meetings:
>
> - individual supervision – staff have the opportunity to review the work they are doing ie any difficulties they are experiencing, any changes they feel they want to implement in their care plans with the children.
>
> - team meetings. Staff meet as a team on a monthly basis. This enables discussion for each nursery team and to share views on how they feel they are working as a team, any changes they as a team feel they need to make.
>
> - staff meetings. They are held on a fortnightly basis. Meetings give staff and management time to review any issues throughout the nursery. Staff discussion group talks take place fortnightly to encourage establishment and staff development. Although each nursery room has its own activity rota and a staff rota these have to be flexible to meet the needs of the children and parents.
>
> We aim every day to provide equipment to develop skills in the following areas and extending play if necessary. We do imaginative play, sand out every day, creative activities, manipulative play, books, gross motor, construction, music, premaths and socialization.

I cautiously ask to see examples of plans. The OIC spends time producing another chart, and two days later hands me the following:

> April. Colour yellow. Nursery rhyme = Humpty Dumpty, Baa Baa Black sheep. Five little ducks; mothers day cards; Easter cards. Spring = animals, pets, planting cress, sunflower seeds [*but there was no evidence of seeds having been planted*].
>
> May/June. Colour green. Transport. Wheels on the bus. Car.

Train. Boat. Fathers day. Visit to airport or ferry or train (*but all visits had been cancelled because of fears of child abuse*).

July/August. Colour blue. Seaside theme. Fish, shells, seaweed etc. Visit to seaside [ditto no visits].

My requests for information, however tentative I try to appear, precipitate a great deal of unease on the part of the OIC, since they expose her claims to provide an educational environment. A further incident again inadvertently exposes the low expectations this nursery holds about the children and parents who attend. At the time of my visit there is an extraordinary art show sponsored by the BBC in the local community, where a group of local people from the housing estate had been taken to visit and select their favourite works of art from national and private collections, which were then loaned to the community to display in local venues including the community centre, the pub and in an empty flat. One of the mothers using the nursery who has some kind of art diploma has been closely involved in this project and talks to me about it with enthusiasm, describing her own and her 3-year-old's favourite picture by Paula Rego. When I relay this conversation to the OIC, she expresses great surprise and says 'social services never told me about this' and that the mother is 'a poor shy wee scrap – who would have believed it?' and that the child 'never spoke to anyone'. The OIC's expectation – first of all that this kind of cultural activity is totally beyond the ability or comprehension of the mother or her child; second, that the social services department maintains such a degree of surveillance that they are likely or able to comment on local goings on; and third, that information about the local community should come from the social services department rather than from her own contacts with parents and staff – constitutes a revealing moment to both of us of how far we are apart in our understanding of nursery practices.

The food in this nursery is poor. Whereas in the Italian and Spanish nurseries the food is freshly purchased and prepared, nutritiously balanced and usually delicious, the meals here are made of cheap tinned, or defrosted, highly processed food – limp beefburgers, greasy chips and tinned spaghetti hoops for one meal (for which the OIC, by now highly anxious, apologized). There are no fresh fruit or vegetables. Meals are dumped on the table, and dished out for the children in a rather haphazard way. There are no clear routines. On one occasion the food is left to get cold, because the children are not properly organized to get to the table. Many of the children have messy eating habits and smear food round their faces, but the wash time after the meal was cursory, and traces of the spaghetti remained on several children's cheeks throughout the rest of the day. (The cook was untrained and unimaginative and retired through ill-health shortly after my visit; her replacement was a male cook who was redeployed from an old people's home which had been closed, and found it very difficult to cater for children.) In all the nurseries the budget for food is very low, around 60p per head, and the cooks and the officers in charge struggle to make ends meet, less successfully here than elsewhere.

The staff in the rooms are patient and gentle and show some physical warmth towards the children, some of whom are very difficult and unresponsive. Very occasionally they give a child a kiss, or a cuddle on their lap. They remain unemphatic even when children were very rough or aggressive. On the other hand the range of activities they provide is dull and limited, far more so than in the first nursery. The few books are mostly inappropriate and tatty, the home corner sparsely equipped with a few broken implements. The staff feel that children cannot cope with too much creative activity, with painting or water play, and access to these activities is limited, partly because of space, partly because of fears about the children's behaviour. This nursery has the nicest of all the outside spaces, with landscaped ground and reasonable outside equipment – bikes, barrows, balls, etc. – and when the children are allowed outside, for a brief 20-minute period in the morning and in the afternoon, they become much more autonomous and alert and play more co-operatively.

Nursery 11

Like the other nurseries this is situated on a working-class estate, but is on the edge of a more prosperous suburban area. The building, which is shared with a social work office, is altogether more spacious, solid and better designed than the others, although it is still subject to vandalism and has a barrier of spikes around the roof. Inside there is a large central hall, equipped with soft play mattresses, for use when the children cannot go outside. At one end of the hall is a bar which separates the hall from the kitchen. In this nursery the cook has a more central role; by virtue of her location in the building, and because of her long service in it, she is a witness to and a commentator on all the events of the nursery. She dishes out cups of tea and coffee to the staff and parents over the bar, and is an invaluable informant to everyone in the nursery (she also takes pride in her menus).

There is a suite of rooms at the other end of the nursery, including the social work office, an OAP luncheon club, interview rooms for the weekly doctor's visit and for other visitors, and a room for parents and toddlers, and for childminders who also use the equipment in the hall. The rooms for the children are larger than in other UK nurseries (although considerably smaller than any of the Italian nurseries), and have a bank of storage cupboards at one end, and a glass wall with window seats and a door to the outside at the other. Each room has its own well maintained adjacent bathroom area. The rooms are carpeted. There are cosy book corners and a wide range of equipment, some of it old and well cared for, some more recent, not all of it appropriate. I attempt to do a geometric matching game, which has been set out for the children one afternoon. It is old and has been in the nursery for many years. I am unable to copy the shapes illustrated on the cover. I say to the nursery worker that I find it difficult, and I wonder if the children can complete it. She shrugs – she has not noticed, she just puts it out as a change of toy.

In this nursery the officer in charge and her deputy regard it as their job to be on the floor as much as possible with the children, and they are skilled practitioners at the service of their staff. The OIC spends much of her time in the baby room, since this is where the most pressure is, due to the recently changed policies of the administration.

There are four group rooms, with two staff to a room, with senior staff available when needed for advice or cover. The staff are more formal with each other and with the children in this nursery. They wear uniforms, and the children address them as aunty. They are a long-serving and close-knit staff group of mainly older women and find changes hard to accommodate. But their stability means they are very at ease in their work. They have even less written planning material than in the other nurseries, but in the room in which I am observing, the skill of the staff is greater.

As with all the other nurseries, I spend most of my time with the 3-year-olds. The school holidays have begun and there are fewer children. The numbers fluctuate between 8 and 11 in the group, always with the same two staff – unlike the other nurseries. There are some distraught and at-risk children, but fewer of them. There are also a number of children from student families, Taiwanese and Indian. These children at first had had no English but are now reasonably articulate. The staff say they did not really help settle in these children, other than carry on with their usual routines: 'Well, they cried a lot at first but its amazing how quickly they pick it [the language] up.'

Uniquely in this nursery the peer group is regarded as having some importance, and there is a discourse about it:

> They [the children] are conscious of being part of a group. They support each other.

> They need to make the most of their childhood, its short enough. They get bored with adult company.

One child in the group had callipers, and according to the member of staff 'they know when she is coming, they make allowances for her, the children will make sure the tables and chairs are in the right position so she can get past'. Lunchtimes were seen as an opportunity for friends to sit together, and on one day there are discussions between the staff and children about who is John's friend because his best friend is away at the moment. Friendships are encouraged amongst the children, and the children do play together more consistently on their own and for longer periods than in the other nurseries.

In particular they play for long periods outside, where they are given more freedom to engage in their own groups and activities. Some of the outside play equipment is designed so that it has to be used by more than one child at a time – bikes with trailers, carts. The permanent outside equipment has been vandalized, but the staff drag out bikes, blankets, books, barrels and planks for balancing, a large cube for hiding in. Groups of children have tea outside on their blankets. The children watch fascinated through the windows when men come with a machine to cut the grass. There is an intermittent commentary between the staff and children, about why the men have come, what they are doing, and how long they will be, whether they will clear up after themselves. The men are from a local day centre, and wave and made faces at the children.

The outside play is inventive as well as physical. Allowing children to be spontaneous is legitimate practice in this nursery. When the children go outside after the grass is cut, they play games about garden maintenance. One girl strides along in a hard hat, ordering her companion to do various odd jobs: 'Come on, I'll be foreman.' Another child lies down on the ground underneath a truck, mending it with his Lego spanner. Others scrummage on the ground for grass cuttings. Some children are dragging a pram with an assortments of odds and ends for a 'boot sale'. One child finds a feather and hands it to her 'aunty' who puts it in her hair and says she is an eagle, and to their delight, chases the flock of little bird-children around.

The children spend hours at a time outside. When the weather is bad, the hall is used as an alternative providing it is not being used by one of the other groups, the parents or toddlers, or the childminders.

In the group room, one 'aunty' was a talented conversationalist, and managed to have long conversations with children, and made a point of doing so with those children who found speech difficult. Dean who has a very limited vocabulary, plays a game of shopping with her. He brings a basket over and signals that he wants to go shopping: 'As long as you've got the bread and potatoes, oh, I'll tell you what some red apples, not green ones, I don't like the green ones.' Dean murmurs something indecipherable and goes to look for apples. He comes back: 'OK, if the greengrocer hasn't got them, I'll get them at the post office. Do you know where the post office is?' Dean says something like 'Up the street'. 'Well, if you are going up the street, don't forget to cross at the lights.' Dean walks across the room and stops at some imaginary lights. He comes back: 'Good job you're here to do the shopping for me. Now what else do I need . . . ' This game goes on for more than 20 minutes, until they are interrupted by another child.

The tone of the conversation is matter of fact and easy going – these are friends playing a game together – unlike the first nursery where the room leader spoke to the children in a high monotonous voice, as if they were simpletons. Such sustained interchanges between adults and children do not occur in any of the other nurseries.

Lunchtime is also a conversational time. 'How does the potato get in the chip?' leads to a discussion about vegetables and fruit, about whether they grow under the ground, on the ground or in trees. The mysteries of food production are pursued later in the afternoon when children make cakes. They go to the kitchen to get the ingredients from the cook, marge, eggs, flour, sugar and milk, and then take the cake they have prepared back to the cook to put in the oven.

In the room where I am observing, the practice in this nursery is more sophisticated and skilled than in any other of the UK nurseries I am investigating (although of course the differences are relative – and there is nothing like the sustained skilled teaching or affection and warmth I have seen in Italian or Spanish nurseries). The district in which the nursery is located is calmer, the officer in charge is more thoughtful and more highly regarded by her staff; the staff themselves are relaxed and competent; the premises are better; the children easier; the support – from the social workers and from the doctor who visits weekly – is readily available; the rapport with parents who come and use the facilities is closer. These factors are cumulative, and one enhances the other. In the last nursery the reverse is the case. Everything is weighted against good practice.

Nursery 12

This nursery, like the first, is in a badly vandalized and run-down area and has the bleakest surroundings of any nursery. The nursery had originally been part of a purpose-built residential unit for families who were being given a last chance to improve their parenting before their children were taken into the care of the local authority. The function has changed within the past two years, and part of the building is now boarded up, but according to other groups in the neighbourhood whom I visited, the function of the building is remembered and resented. 'Don't go in there, they'll take your kids off you' is, by their account, a widely held view in the local community. All parts of the building have metal shutters. Doors are padlocked and bolted. A night security guard is employed to protect the building but it is regularly broken into, and on the first day of my visit the security guard himself is locked out by an intruder he is chasing. He has to break in again with a crowbar. Staff express fear about coming to work or leaving in the dark. Every morning the staff have to do a check of grounds for used condoms, needles, broken glass and other debris. Inside the nursery it is dark because of the shuttering. The kitchen is the worst room – it is tiny and its skylight has been boarded up. There is no other source of light or air and the staff worked under florescent lighting and without ventilation. Other rooms, the group rooms, the staffrooms and office, are scruffy and uncared for, with battered furniture and scuffed paint. The displays are tatty, and have been there a long time. Equipment is worn, and meagre storage cupboards contain a jumble of material. The rooms have their own adjacent bathrooms, but the staff share a toilet with the children and it is not clean.

The nursery is a 40-place nursery, currently operating at a capacity of 36. Of these children, 11 are on the at-risk register and/or have some kind of special needs diagnosis. Some of these children are extremely distraught and unkempt. One of the 3-year-olds is encopretic and soils himself continually. Another disturbed child is an extremely abusive 4-year-old: 'You bastard, you fucking nutter, you stupid cow' is his refrain. Two of the girls who are more articulate take his language in their stride and laugh, but other children are upset by his continual abuse and avoid him or try to hide from him in the yard.

There are also a group of Arabic-speaking children, mainly Somali, and a few Nigerian children, from student families who, in contrast to other children, arrive at the nursery neatly and smartly dressed, and carefully groomed. A Somali worker has been hired, but she does not work with the Arabic-speaking children and rarely intervenes on their behalf. She says that the parents want their children to learn English, and she is reluctant to interpret for them. These children form a subgroup within the nursery. They avoid the other children, whose language they do not understand, and whose behaviour is obviously threatening. They tend to play with each other in the courtyard or else do not interact at all. One 3-year-old is completely isolated and does not speak or interact with anyone, neither staff nor other children, but no one appears to notice his isolation.

The OIC produces a newly typewritten sheet which describes the overall goal of the nursery as 'to work in partnership with parents in providing a family support service which promoted the health and wellbeing of children, recognized the needs of all family members and positively promotes equal opportunities.' This overall goal is broken down into four separate aims:

- to provide quality flexible daycare for children under 5 years
- to provide facilities where families can meet for recreational purposes
- to provide safe play facilities
- to provide information, advice and guidance to families with young children.

The daily organization in the nursery is chaotic, particularly in the group of 3-year-olds, where one of the nursery workers, a

powerful personality, has such an erratic and inconsistent style
that I am concerned for the children. The room is dirty and scruffy,
the few toys are broken, the equipment mixed up, bits of paper
and styrofoam are left on the floor. The nursery worker wanders
in and out of the room without saying where she is going or for
how long. She continually redresses her hair and changes her
make-up, and this grooming she carries out in the room as well
as outside it, with complete disregard of her situation, and obliv-
ious to everyone she is with, other staff and children alike. She is
airily off hand with the children. She is not deliberately unkind
but she does not appear in any way to be engaged. For instance
the cook brings in a morning snack of cocoa and biscuits. The
worker takes the tray in and dumps it on the top of a storage
shelf. She does not attempt to get children to sit down, or to
monitor who has and has not had a drink. She just says to no one
in particular 'It's here'. Some children cautiously take a drink,
others ignore it (lunchtimes are slightly better, since one of the
rooms is used as a dining room and children from the oldest two
groups eat together with their staff).

Suddenly this nursery worker barks instructions at children,
and then ignores what she has said. She tells the children to do
something then forgets what it is she has asked. She says, 'Now
we are going to make a picture,' and puts some paper and a
few scraps on the floor. One child sticks on a bit of tinsel
and then wonders off. The worker then says 'We're going next
door to watch the video' and without saying anything else
about the picture, and leaving it on the floor, shoos the children
next door. She takes time off in the afternoon to finish the
picture on her own, and next day the picture, with more tinsel
stuck on it in a pattern, is pinned to the wall with a caption
'We made this picture with tinsel'. She shows me the picture the
next day and comments that working with young children is
'hard work'.

Later I comment that the Arabic-speaking child seems quite isolated and has great difficulty in communicating either to staff or
to other children. She laughs and says the child has 'excellent language'. In this room each day I come the children watch videos
of cartoons for up to six hours a day. The deputy OIC hovers anx-
iously at the door, and tries to get the children to go out. She does
manage to get the children into the playground when the worker
is taking a lunch break and a tea break. But when the children
come in the video is put on again.

Despite it being one of the central aims of the nursery to work with parents, only one parent, in the baby room, reluctantly stays in the nursery. No one consults the staff during my visit. Parents and children are not greeted on arrival or departure. I speak to one Nigerian parent who comes to collect her child (to the refrain of 'you fucking bastard' from the 4-year-old): 'I am itching to go back [to Nigeria]. So what is the enjoyment of life without your friends and relatives. This is not a good place to be. So many things have happened here.'

When I ask about parent participation I am shown photos of a past summer picnic with the parents, but no events had been organized for parents for some time because of the stress of the vandalism. The information leaflets which were displayed for parents were badly out of date.

The OIC is a nurse with an additional qualification in community work, but he has had no previous experience with young children and he rarely visits the rooms or speaks to the children. He has organized many *ad hoc* training sessions and team-building sessions for the staff – speech therapy, High Scope, stress management, aromatherapy. The fact that the nursery is so far from realizing its aims that they amount to fantasy, and that training has so little effect, suggest that the demoralization of the staff is severe; but also that the officer in charge does not know what he is doing. (He left a few months later.)

As with one of the Italian nurseries, I was shocked by the quality of care offered. I recommended that the nursery be closed, since not only was it very expensive to maintain, given the security bill, but on balance it also appeared to be doing the children more harm than good. In Italy and Spain I was visiting strictly in the capacity of an observer and not in a position to do anything except to make mild comments. In the UK city I then became involved in the development of the service. As I go on to explain in the last chapter this service has changed considerably and is now better managed, and the above nursery, although not closed, has fortunately been revamped and reorganized.

This chapter has attempted to provide portraits of each of the nurseries in the study. One of the aims of the study was to see what differences if any could be attributed to collective working. In reality the question turns out to have been too simplistic. There are all kinds of influences and ideas being played out, although it is possible to claim broadly that the nurseries with the busiest and happiest children had a coherent and thoughtful approach which was shared and articulated by all staff members and it was more difficult to achieve this coherence in a hierarchical setting. In the next chapter these influences and ideas are explored further.

6

Love and Friendship
in the Nursery

Love has no position
Love's a way of living
One kind of relation
Possible between
Any things or persons
Given one condition
The one sine qua non
Being mutual need
(W. H. Auden)

What conclusions can we draw from this study? Are there factors which can be identified as supporting 'good' nursery provision? Are there other factors which make 'good' nurseries very hard to achieve?

The first and most obvious point to make is that all the nurseries in this study think they are doing a good job. Even the nursery which was most disastrous, working with distraught children in a vandalized building with chaotic routines, had self-evaluation sessions where staff reviewed their progress favourably. Paradoxically those nurseries which had achieved the highest standards, and had most closely fulfilled the aims and objectives they had set themselves – the Italian nursery which was so attentive to individual children, and the two Spanish nurseries where children were so positively encouraged to learn – were more self-critical, or at least had a process of continuous collective review and redefinition of what they wanted to achieve. This suggests that self-evaluation, although important is not sufficient. How do these perceptions or misperceptions happen? What produces low aspirations and complacency on the one hand, and on the other hand, high aspirations and continual effort?

The conclusion I have drawn is banal: that a 'good' nursery, however defined, does not exist in isolation; that it is a part of a multifaceted web of values and practices. This is what Bronfenbrenner called an 'ecological' approach (although ecological theory is too general to use as a means of prediction in this case). Whilst the skills, aptitudes and training of those working with children (and their pay and job security); the management and organization of the nursery; the curriculum or range of activities which is offered to children; the resources which are available – all determine daily practice, they are necessary but not sufficient criteria. Staff in nurseries ultimately judge themselves by locating their practice against what they see to be the current professional, parental and public perceptions of their work, and where those expectations are minimal, then the nurseries in turn do not provide very much.

In this chapter I have tried to draw out some of the levels and strands of influence on nursery practice and to clarify some of the issues involved.

Social cohesion

The nurseries in this study were all within or on the outskirts of major industrial cities. But the experiences of young children within those cities was very different. In the region of northern Italy the level of prosperity, the way in which prosperity was shared out between citizens, the stability and homogeneity of the community, and the rich cultural traditions, dating back to the Renaissance, meant that it was a secure and very pleasant place in which to grow up. The Spanish city offered a different context, a more dramatic political history, greater extremes of wealth and poverty, a more heterogeneous community, but also one with powerful cultural traditions. The UK city had a badly eroded industrial base, and social cohesion had broken down in those parts of the city which were working-class ghettos. Riots, vandalism and drugtaking were commonplace, poverty was widespread, and levels of crime were high. There was little in the way of a distinctive cultural heritage. For many children, this city was a threatening and dismal place in which to grow up.

It is beyond the remit of this book to discuss the macroeconomic policies which have given rise to such disparities. However it is clear that the role played by any nursery in influencing these events is marginal. Instead, the nurseries inevitably reflect the wider social and political climate and in their way, and in turn, contribute to it. In the Italian region most people were in work, and the aspirations of workers, parents and children were confident and buoyant despite recent political events. In Spain, the opportunities to develop the service reflected both recent political initiatives and drew upon long-standing local democratic traditions – to put this crudely, those involved in the service were hopeful that change and development would continue to occur. In the UK city there was widespread unemployment, and expectations were minimal – that the next day would not be worse than the previous one. No more redundancies or cut-backs in services would be announced, no more vandalism or break-ins would have taken place, no more cases of child abuse would be uncovered. In the period when I was conducting the study, a major employer went bankrupt and a further 2,000 jobs were lost; there was a serious child abuse scandal and a so-called 'paedophile ring' was suspected; and there were break-ins and fires on the estates where three of the nurseries were situated.

These situations are not permanent. Political situations fluctuate, economic trends vary, local initiatives combat national trends. But at the time of the study, the difference in macroeconomic circumstances in each of the areas where the investigation took place was marked, and this inevitably had an effect on the service provided.

Policies for early childhood services

In Italy whilst there had been a series of laws passed about services, the initiative to develop services was a regional one. The region of Emilia-Romagna has a particularly high standard of provision, with around 40% of children 0–3 in daycare. The services have a generous infrastructure, and have been the subject of discussion, debate and research for the last 20–30 years (Corsaro and Emiliani, 1992). Educational philosophers such as Bruno Ciari (1982 quoted in Lamb *et al.*, 1992, p. 91)) argued that preprimary education was a means of giving every child, regardless of background 'a common cultural foundation on which to grow as a person and citizen'. This philosophy was not only widely accepted by those who used and worked in the services but was also more generally espoused by the community at large. Nurseries are an important and valued service.

The nurseries who took part in this study were also part of a broader initiative sponsored by the regional research institute (IRPA) to look at the role of co-ordinators in supporting collective nurseries, and in particular to explore the ideas of Loczy, a Hungarian system of encouraging independence and autonomy in young children. All the nurseries in this study were therefore part of a wider climate of discussion and research, and there were sophisticated information systems, and a familiarity with and a willingness to engage in debate about the function and practices of services.

In Spain there was a new national policy, LOGSE, which recast thinking about children 0–6 and emphasized the educational nature of the service. Whilst the take-up of this national initiative has not been uniform (Valiente, 1995), in Barcelona it had been enthusiastically developed. There were many reference documents, discussions and meetings which explored the context of the new legislation. Above all there had been an emphasis on in-service training, so that within less than 10 years, from having had few formal qualifications, 80% of the workforce had become trained. At a city level there were very high expectations of what nurseries might achieve, and a continual definition and redefinition of good practice – of which this research is a small part.

The policy framework in the UK derived from the Children Act 1989, which aimed to provide 'family support' and daycare services for 'children in need'. At a local level this policy was not further clarified or discussed, and it was implicitly accepted at the time of the investigation that the day nurseries were a social work resource for particularly vulnerable families, which stressed care, surveillance and family harmony. The nurseries were not seen primarily as a place where children learn.

Yet even though staff in UK nurseries were dealing with the most deprived members of an already deprived community, they received less rather than more support than their fellow workers in Italy and Spain. They worked longer hours, had fewer holidays and were less likely to be well trained, and were considerably less likely to take part in in-service training. The administration expected very little of the staff. They were operating in a small and neglected area of social welfare and what was provided for the children was regarded as less important than understanding of and involvement in the broader system of social services – hence the appointment of one of the officers in charge who had no qualification in and no experience of working with young children. No one would employ a person without structural engineering qualifications to build a bridge; but working in publicly funded services in the UK with young children requires no such expertise. Professional expectations of what work might be undertaken with young children focused almost entirely on the social rehabilitation of their families. When asked what ambitions they had for themselves, most staff that sought further training or promotion said that they wished to specialize more in working with damaged and stressed children and their families.

In these circumstances it can be seen that whereas in Spain and Italy there was a positive view of a nursery as being able to offer developmental experiences for children, and continuous discussion about how it might be done, in the UK there was relatively little expectation or discussion about how children spent their time in a day nursery.

Initial and continuous training

The requirements for staff training are a further indication of the policy importance and weighting of early years services. In Italy the national requirements were contradictory. In practice most of those entering nursery work in the *asilo nido* had a two-year post-16 vocational qualification, although some staff did have degrees in sociology or psychology. The Italian region regarded this vocational training as inadequate, and aimed to compensate for it by providing a comprehensive in-service training programme, and six hours per week were designated non-contact time, mostly spent on training, meetings and seminars.

In Spain LOGSE also reorganized tertiary training, and many universities set up three-year post-18 teacher training courses for those working with children 0–6, entry to which could be gained either through a vocational or non-vocational route. LOGSE stipulated that those in charge of infant schools for children 0–3 should have such a qualification, but Barcelona interpreted this requirement more stringently, and as stated above, 80% of staff in the nurseries now held this qualification. A few already had degrees. Initial training stressed the potential for education and learning for small children, and was heavily practice based, so that staff were able to build up a substantial repertoire of pedagogic activities during their training. In addition, six hours per week were also designated as non-contact time.

In the UK the standard requirement for working in publicly funded daycare is a nursery nurse qualification known as NNEB, a two-year post-16 vocational qualification. There is considerable ambivalence over this qualification. Unions argue that it is a substantial professional qualification covering the age range 0–6 or 0–8 and an important opportunity for many working-class women who might otherwise remain unqualified to become professionalized. On the other hand, teachers are required to undertake four years' post-18 academic study, and compared with the standard expected of teachers, the NNEB qualification is barely sufficient to gain entry to a teacher training course. In the education sector nursery nurses can only work as teachers' assistants in nursery schools and classes for 3–5-year-old children, whereas in the social services sector, they are entirely responsible for managing the nurseries and for providing a service to the more difficult children and families who are referred to the nurseries.

The NNEB therefore is a short basic training, but because of low expectations of what daycare services might provide, it is not only regarded as an adequate training but outside the education system it is also regarded as being of good professional standing. Moreover in-service or continuous training is not routinely provided. In the UK nurseries it was expected that if staff sought further training or qualifications it would be at almost entirely their own expense and in their own time. Not surprisingly few staff undertook such training. The result was that having obtained their NNEB, staff regarded their training as having finished. The staffrooms contained no books or resource materials, and their was no culture of training and development, either at an individual or at a nursery level.

The organization of the nurseries

The Italian and Spanish nurseries were organized as collectives. There were no managers, and staff made their decisions as a group. In the Italian nurseries, a co-ordinator was responsible for a group of 8–10 nurseries, and was in effect their manager. The co-ordinator acting within the terms of reference of the local administration took the important decisions about finance, about admissions, about aims and objectives, about curriculum and within the concourse system, about staffing. But within these boundaries the staff were self-organizing and all members of staff on the site were equal and valued their egalitarianism.

The Spanish nurseries were more autonomous, and took most of these important decisions for themselves. They elected one of the collective to serve as the administrator, but emphasized that this post conferred no special status or remuneration. They also emphasized the burden that this collective way of working entailed, but were also clear about the benefits that accrued.

In both Italy and Spain this egalitarian way of working was seen as unexceptional, and drew on much wider historical and co-operative traditions. It was not seen as unusual, and no special skills or training were required to work in this way. It was simply how the nurseries were organized. Because collective practices were normal, there were no obvious informal leaders or power struggles as has happened with the few fraught experiments with collectives in the UK, in the 1960s and 1970s when breaking away from a hierarchical system proved extremely problematic (Stanton, 1989). In Italy and Spain collective working was a well tried way of working with which staff felt comfortable. It was reinforced by social practices – daily communal meals, and frequent outings and celebrations.

In the UK however, the nurseries were hierarchically organized. There were nine grades of staff, each grade carrying a different status and remuneration. There was considerable rhetoric about management and management skills. The officer-in-charge was very much in charge, and although some of the rhetoric concerned inclusive styles of management, there was no question about the decisions of the officer-in-charge being over-ruled. Often they were not even discussed. In one of the nurseries for instance, staff were changed around between rooms, and one was even transferred to another nursery, because the officer-in-charge decided it would be better for the members of staff concerned, but their permission was not sought. This hierarchical approach permeated the system. The officers-in-charge in turn deferred their decisions to a nursery manager, who in turn deferred hers to an assistant director of social services whose main function concerned residential services to the elderly. Decision-making was continually referred up and down the system by means of written instructions. Where such a hierarchical system existed and so much power was invested in individual managers, then the quality of the management was important. A good manager who worked democratically with her staff and was an experienced practitioner could influence the practice in the nursery. A poor manager by the same token would have an adverse effect. There were no social practices which counteracted this hierarchy. There were no communal mealtimes, and communal outings or other events were rare. The friendships of the nursery rarely spilled over into non-working time.

Premises and resources

The workplace itself exercises an influence on practice. Freire (1996) coined the phrase 'pedagogical space' to describe the working conditions of teachers. He argued that for the staff, the space was like an extension of home. If you cared about your surroundings you cared about what went on inside them; and conversely, ill-cared for spaces were a sign that the educators themselves were disregarded and undervalued. Very generally this seemed to be true, although, as with all these aspects of services, each strand or aspect of provision contributes to the overall picture. It was possible to have a very generously provided workplace, as with one of the Italian nurseries, yet use it badly; or to have a very poor workplace, as with two of the Spanish nurseries, but use it well.

The Spanish nurseries were the best equipped. They provided a much wider and more imaginative range of activities for children, with more original materials, even when the premises were unsatisfactory.

In the UK nurseries the security of the premises was a paramount consideration. Each of them regularly experienced vandalism, graffiti and break-ins. In one of them it was a weekly occurrence. The buildings, with one exception, offered limited space, and all were poorly equipped in comparison with the Spanish nurseries, but also in comparison with neighbouring nursery classes within the education system.

These aspects of provision, premises and equipment, are a reflection of the general esteem in which the service is held and the resources which are deemed appropriate; but they are also a reflection of the aims and objectives and curriculum of the nursery – ideas about what children do in the nursery, how they pass their time, and what is expected of them.

Curriculum

Expectations about what the children might do during the day varied with each nursery. In the Spanish nurseries, children were seen as active and eager learners, and the activities were organized in such a way as to promote learning and extend knowledge. In one case, this had resulted in a didactic regime, where children were instructed beyond their capacity to respond. In another the activities were perfectly pitched so as to extend children's learning to a remarkable degree but this required an extraordinary degree of energy and attention on the part of the staff. In yet another nursery, the sociability and conviviality of the regime were the spur to learning. But in all of them, learning was a *raison d'être*, a framework set by the legislation, endorsed and promoted by the municipality, and made achievable through the initial and continuous training of the staff and the resourcing of the nurseries.

In the Italian nurseries, there was less emphasis on learning and more on the emotional autonomy of the child. In one of the Italian nurseries the absence of a focus on learning meant that the staff provided very little in the way of activities for the children, who were bored and fractious. But where the notion of autonomy was most carefully worked out, then the responses to each child were superbly and meticulously judged, again requiring a remarkable amount of effort on the part of the staff.

In the UK nurseries, inevitably given all the other constraints, very little was expected of children, and not much was provided for them. It was the absence of any coherent ideas that was so striking – nobody had thought very much about what children could or might do. There was no written material circulated, no discussion, no thoughtful planning. There were care plans for individual children which focused on their family relationships; and there was a ready-made system of assessment, the Portage system which offered a chart by which children's developmental milestones could be measured, but this bore little relation to what was going on in the rooms, and was infrequently used, or not used at all, for most children. One or two individual members of staff displayed a flair for their work, and supported and challenged the children in their behaviour and thinking, but in comparison with the standards achieved in the best of the Spanish and Italian nurseries, the UK nurseries were dismal indeed.

Physical well-being

In the UK nurseries health and safety were an overwhelming consideration. There was what amounted to an obsession with safety features, with any potentially dangerous materials being removed from the immediate environment. In particular kitchens were out of bounds˙ (although in one of the nurseries it was possible to relax this rule slightly) and the outside play spaces were unadventurous. Children were given little opportunity to extend themselves physically or to anticipate any hazards. Because of an incident in another nursery, not included in the study, no one who was not thoroughly vetted by the police was allowed near children – including ancillary staff – and no children were allowed on outings.

One of the Italian nurseries too was obsessed with hygiene and with keeping the nursery clean – a circumstance reinforced by the generous nature of the contracts to ancillary staff, where even a supply window-cleaner was produced.

By contrast the Spanish nurseries, particularly in the older buildings, were almost cavalier about health and safety regulations. But this was compensated for by a view that children had to learn for themselves about the hazards of the environment, and it was the job of the staff to help them learn and to protect them whilst they were learning.

But unlike the narrow view of health and safety in the UK, in which the priority was to avoid any physical danger and to eliminate any physical risk or challenge, both the Italian and Spanish nurseries had a broader concept of 'well-being'. This meant making sure that children had regular routines, that they ate well, rested well, and exercised well. This concept was almost entirely lacking from the UK nurseries. The children did not attend regularly, and rarely for the whole day, so they did not have reliable and secure routines. They often appeared tired but there was nowhere comfortable or quiet to lie down and rest in any of the rooms. They ate in the nursery, but this, like almost everything else was a preventative measure to make sure they ate a certain quantity of food, rather than a pleasurable meal to be savoured. Because the outside area was generally considered hazardous, and the children were potentially out of control when they used it, they went outside for infrequent periods, and had to move carefully in the cramped rooms. Only in one of the UK nurseries did the children begin to exert themselves, to use their limbs in imaginative and exploratory ways, and to test and extend their bodily co-ordination. The level of exercise and physical extension that was commonplace in the nurseries in Italy and Spain did not often occur in a UK context.

Individual children

The nurseries, whatever the circumstances in which they operate, are places where children spend their time, and it is by their effect on individual children that they must ultimately be judged. It is not a simple matter, and depends, as we have seen, on the aims and objectives of the nursery, and on the expectations of the society of which it is a part.

In the Anglo-American literature the needs of an individual are often posed as being *against* those of the group. Group care is for those who cannot be looked after as individuals. In Italy and Spain however, group care is seen as a way in which *the individual*, even a very young child, can more fully realize his or her potential. This approach has been most fully articulated by the Italian educator Malaguzzi (1993, p. 11): 'The organization of small-group work is much more than a simple functional tool; it is a cultural context that contains within itself a vitality and an infinite network of possibilities.'

In the UK nurseries children were seen only as an aggregation of individuals. However, as I have stressed, all these aspects are interlinked, and the poor care received by the UK nurseries was a consequence of many interacting factors, not just the failure to understand how groups function.

Love and friendship in the nursery

One critical factor seemed to be the level of attention and devotion of the staff to the children with whom they were working – love and friendship I have called it in this chapter. As Judy Dunn (1993, p. 109) has suggested, the nature of friendship, its continuity and reciprocity, is a transforming experience: 'Friends can create a world of great involvement and high adventure . . . they must co-ordinate their efforts with all the virtuosity of an accomplished jazz quartet and they must manage the amount of conflict between them. This requires enormous social skill.'

Friendship, she suggests, may not only be a feature of

child–child relationships but also a paradigm for adult–child relationships. Viewed in this way, many of the children I observed – Carlo and David in the Italian nurseries, Marco in the Spanish nursery, Dean in the UK nursery – were experiencing the joys of friendship, affection, enjoyment, caring and support, the creation of an exciting and distinctive world, in their interactions with staff.

But there are some children who find these interactions much more difficult than others, either because of a disability or because of a language barrier, or because of damaging experiences before they come to nursery. Such children need particular attention and support. It is not sufficient to treat all children alike because they are patently not alike and a skilled nursery worker needs to have some understanding of how they differ and why and what to do about it – an understanding of an individual child but one which does not lose sight of the restorative powers of being in a group. In some of the nurseries this sensitivity and balance were superbly developed, but in others it was rudimentary.

To paraphrase Malaguzzi (1993, p. 10), love and friendship is a motor for development:

> Our image of children no longer considers them as isolated and egocentric, does not only see them engaged in action with objects, does not emphasize only the cognitive aspects, does not belittle feelings or what is not logical, and does not consider with ambiguity the role of the affective domain. Instead our image of the child is rich in potential, strong, powerful, competent, and most of all, connected to adults and other children.

Conclusion

I began the chapter by saying that it is impossible to consider 'good practice' in isolation: it is part of a complex web of values and assumptions, and in understanding why nurseries differ from one another, particularly when making international comparisons, it is necessary to examine a whole range of issues, many if not most of which lie outside the control or influence of the individual nursery or individual member of staff.

Yet in similar settings the nurseries did differ from one another and the staff did behave differently. In the Italian sample, the differences between the nurseries were considerable. In two of the nurseries the attention that was paid to the children was careful and caring and well planned; but in one of the nurseries the situation had somehow become out of hand, and the staff did not see what to me as an observer seemed obvious, that children were restless and unhappy because their room was so barren and there was so little for them to do in it.

In the Spanish sample, the concentration on the children as learners, had in one case led to the didactic approach. Children as young as 3 are not ready for formal instruction. But again where this emphasis on learning was tempered with love and friendship, the nurseries were very good and one of the nurseries was a particularly merry and life-giving place to be.

Even in the UK nurseries, operating in a much more difficult and negative climate, there were considerable differences. One of the nurseries, admittedly better resourced than the others, did have a committed and experienced manager to lead it, and the nursery offered the children more fun and friendship, more freedom and more consistency than in the other nurseries. Gifted individual staff shine although the chances of remaining untarnished by the system are limited.

In an egalitarian society, with national and local policy frameworks on early years services, with generous and well re-sourced levels of provision reflecting the needs of the local community, with well trained staff who are able to review and revise their work through continuous training, with support from expert practitioners and researchers, with a concern for children's physical well-being and a well planned curriculum, and with sensitivity to vulnerable children, then nurseries can be sociable and stimulating places, and the staff working in them can blossom, fulfil their own potential as educators and carers, and by doing so enhance the lives of the children with whom they work – and in turn be enhanced by them. The best nurseries are part of a civic and civilizing enterprise.

7

Postscript: Making changes in the UK

New ways of valuing and thinking do not become instituted from one day to the next, like magic. It is not like moving a table from one spot in the house to another, in which physical strength is all that is required. Changing cultural habits is a different story.

(Paulo Freire)

In this chapter I go beyond description into polemic and prescription, because it is clear that by comparison with what happens to young children in nurseries in Italy and Spain, something is badly wrong in the UK. I have no reason to suppose the situations I have described are untypical. Many colleagues engaged in administration or in research and consultancy in the daycare field have made similar comments to me, and have described circumstances much like those included here. Being in a day nursery in the UK is frequently a painful and constricting experience for the staff and for the children alike. It is not much of an exaggeration to say this situation is scandalous.

In the time since this research has been carried out there has been a considerable investment in the day nurseries in the particular UK local authority described in this book, and more is being planned. Some of the senior staff have been replaced, and the daycare service itself is being reorganized and closer links are being forged with education services. The research described here was one of a number of catalysts which prompted change, although by no means the major one, and I have been privileged as a researcher to continue my involvement. The changes which have been instituted have been very gradual, and there is still a long way to go. As Freire (1996) says about his own famous attempts directing education and literacy programmes in Brazil, new ways of working require a long, sustained and participatory effort. Change, if it is to take root, is a slow process, and the obstacles are many.

What kind of changes are necessary to publicly funded day nurseries in the UK and how can they be made? The reasons for the poor practice I have described are complex, and there are many explanations which can be provided. What is clear is that it is not a failure of the individuals who work in the nurseries – their struggle to provide a decent service is in some cases heroic. On the contrary it represents a failure of the system at every level, from the theoretical, to the political, to the practical. Whilst this failure affects publicly funded day nurseries the most, because of where they are sited, and because the most vulnerable children attend them, the comments about practice which follow are also relevant to nursery practice in private day nurseries, or family centres, and to a lesser extent and in a different way to nursery education.

The poverty of theory

What was lacking in the UK day nurseries above all was any ability by most of the staff to explain and analyse what they were doing. They had no articulated rationale for their practices, only half-remembered and ill-digested ideas about child development and learning and attachment theory. This is partly because of poor initial training and partly because of the absence of any time allowed for continuous or in-service training. But I would argue this was mainly because there was no theory of pedagogy on which they could draw. What should children be doing in nurseries? How is that different from the way they learn or behave at home? The Italian and Spanish nurseries had such theories and from day to day they were trying to test them against practice, however well or badly they did it. As Freire (1996, p. 108) observes:

> Practice needs theory and theory needs practice just like a fish needs clean water. Practice apart from critical reflection, which illuminates the theory embedded in practice, cannot help our understanding. Revealing the theory embedded in practice undoubtedly helps the subject of practice to understand practice by reflecting and improving on it.

In the UK day nurseries for the most part the activities were a recital of the previous day's practices; there was nothing new to be learnt only repetition and a slight variation of what had gone on before – the rotas of toys for example, which in one nursery meant putting out the Little Tykes plastic playthings on Thursday afternoons; or the elderly geometric puzzle which the children could not manage, and neither could I – it was on the level of an advanced IQ test for adults – yet it had patiently and carefully been preserved and set out at intervals for these 3-year-olds for the last 15 years!

Not only was there no critical idea of what or how children might *learn* in the day nurseries, or what kind of repertoire of activities might be available for them, but there was also no idea about how children might *behave* together. It should have been self-evident that if a stressed and confused 3-year-old child who has the greatest difficulty in relating to other people comes to nursery then it will confuse him or her even more if, on each of the three mornings he or she comes, he or she is with a different group of children. Yet this was the common everyday practice of the nurseries. It was rare for most children to be in the same group of children throughout the week. Far from being self-evident, it had not occurred to anyone that this practice might be damaging to children.

What theoretical perspectives can practitioners refer to? The underpinning knowledge which is required for the new National Vocational Qualification (NVQ) in Childcare and Education, which draws intimately on traditions of nursery nurse training, relies on a watered-down version of child development theory. This sets out developmentally appropriate practice, and gives an explanation of what children can reasonably be expected to do at different ages. But even though it offers insight into the processes of learning, the poverty and irrelevance of theory in child development as a guide to practice are already the subject of soul-searching by some of its most eminent theorists (Kessen, 1983; Bronfenbrenner *et al.*, 1986; Morss, 1990; Lamb *et al.*, 1992; Elder *et al.*, 1993), as well as being criticized as a discipline by those outside it (James and Prout, 1990; Qvortrup *et al.*, 1994; Hood *et al.*, 1996; Mayall, 1996). This angst about child development rests on a number of inter-related grounds: its positivistic and pseudo-scientific methodologies so little of worth can be demonstrated or proved unless it is systematically manipulated in an experimental paradigm and then made quantifiable; its postulation of an invariable sequence of stages through which a child passes on the way to being grown-up; its focus on the individual as the centrepiece; and its ignorance of historical, social and cultural conditions.

Bronfenbrenner *et al.* (1986, p. 1220) who sit midway between orthodox developmentalists and their critics argue that whilst a scientific approach is necessary to check and validate knowledge, admit the whole enterprise of scientific research is value laden: 'Developmental psychology is about the attempt to find values, the attempt to deal with values, and to help people establish values for their work with children. Until we can address, understand, and come to terms with this value-critical, value-normative aspect of our field, we are evading its central issue.' Science in other words is not neutral, and the conclusions of developmental psychologists need themselves to be set in their context and taken with a pinch of salt. 'Facts' cannot be divorced from their method of discovery. Bronfenbrenner still hankers after the scientific method and quantifiable results, however tempered, but some of his colleagues have gone still further. Because of this queasiness about what to do about the richness and variety of the 'real' world, developmental psychologists have, on the one hand, resorted to ever narrower experiments and fields of study, and on the other, begun – slowly – to accept more qualitative methodologies (Ball, 1993). As Elder *et al.* (1993, p. 193) comment: Science's grip on the discipline of psychology has prevented quite the rout of positivism occurring in philosophy and history, but we see a weakening at the edges.'

It is now widely accepted that developmental psychology, however insightful it may be on very particular and refined points (Grieve and Hughes, 1990), is not a coherent field, but a fragmented, and often contradictory mass of findings which do not add up to a picture of what children are or what they can do. As Kessen (1983, p. 26) suggests in a well-known article, the child is not so much a universal phenomenon whose attributes we are gradually coming to understand, but a cultural invention: 'Developmental psychologists seem to have lost a clear sense of where their discipline is going, and part of this reassessment has been the discovery of the "invented" child.'

Following on from the critique that the methods of developmental psychology are based on those of nineteenth-century science, Morss (1990) and Cahan *et al.* (1993) point out that the central understanding of developmental psychology is of a sequence of stages which rests on a biological, and therefore inappropriate, metaphor of development, one which minimizes rather than emphasizes variation, and which takes for granted that psychological or mental functions are an uncomplicated reflection of biological functions – that measuring children's developmental stages is essentially no different from measuring their height or weight:

> Developmental psychologists have searched for natural sequences of ages and stages in the child's understanding of physical, social and moral worlds. Problems have accumulated because this approach has rested, more often than not, upon an exclusively biological orientation. The biological metaphor ignores the social and historical aspects of the child's development and takes them as secondary. The traditional biological approach has been characteristically finalistic, centring attention on what children are to become and concerned with the child's march towards adulthood. Such approaches have ignored the scientific need to understand children as constantly viable; naturally adapted creatures in their own right.
>
> (Cahan *et al.*, 1993, p. 221)

This notion of the universal decontextualized child, against which progress can be measured, rather as height and weight can be measured, is implicit in much of the literature on child development, and in the training materials which are available to those working with young children – for instance the Portage system in common use in the nurseries. As mentioned above, the eminent Harvard psychologist Kessen argues on the contrary that the child is a cultural invention. His argument is both that this approach of developmentally appropriate practice is far too crude in helping us understand what a given child is like and why he or she does what he or she does; and that it diverts our attention away from the present. For example the views of the mother and child who liked the work of the artist Paula Rego (the mother even took part in a television programme where she competently and confidently discussed the pictures with an art critic) were completely outside the comprehension of the nursery officer – there is no category in the Portage system for a child's aesthetic preferences. Teachers and childcarers are trained to think about the next stage, and the one after that, and how it compares with the one before, rather than supporting a child in enjoying the moment. Imagine if our own experiences and daily pleasures were continually judged by a more powerful person – who did not know us very well – in terms of how they might help us change from what we are into something else of which we are only dimly aware.

The third critique is based on what Kessen (1993, p. 227) calls our obsession with individuality: 'We are all driven, obsessed even, by the priority of the individual. The individual remains in the centre of our metaphysics, our ethics, our epistemology and our scholarship.' Even those theorists such as Bronfenbrenner who try to represent the child surrounded by concentric circles of influence – the family, the nursery or school, the local community, the nation state – still see the individual child as the pinpoint in the middle, the lonesome individual whom the world in its various manifestations, presses in on, influences and shapes, in ways it is hoped that are measurable. The Spanish and Italian nurseries have escaped some of this Anglo-American preoccupation with individuality, and the Italian theorist Malaguzzi has in particular tried to articulate a more connected, more collective focus for his analysis of how nurseries function. He has done this to great practical effect. The nurseries in the commune of Reggio Emilia with which he is associated have attracted international professional recognition, and received the popular accolade in *Time* magazine as the best nurseries in the world. Reggio Emilia is now a place of pilgrimage for early years specialists. But as Dahlberg (1995), who has been closely associated with his efforts, suggests much of the admiration is misplaced. It is not so much that Malaguzzi had innovative ideas about learning which enabled children to produce, for example, extraordinary works of art. It is, on the contrary, that he inspired a discourse between staff, parents and children, a democratic dialogue about what it means to act together, to plan and think collectively:

> We strive to create an amiable [nursery] school where children, teachers and families feel a sense of well-being; therefore, the organization of the schools – contents, functions, procedures, motivations, and interests – is designed to bring together the three central protagonists – children, teachers, and parents – and to intensify the inter-relationships among them . . . What is appreciated all along is the shared sense of satisfaction and accomplishment as individuals and as a group.
>
> (*Ibid.*, p. 11)

Again if we go back to our UK nurseries, individualism dominates practice. There is no other rationale, no basis for action when children and adults come together, no sense that the nursery as an organization can or should add anything different or new to the children's daily lives, no sense that the lived experiences are anything more than aggregate of separate and individual reactions. When I prompted, the most articulate explanation that was offered of what the nursery was doing is that staff are trying to make the nursery as much like home as possible – but the presence of a token strip of carpet or an armchair cannot begin to turn an institution for 40 or 50 children into a home; it does not remotely resemble one. In fact it is cut off in its practices from anything ordinary or daily that is going on around it – shopping, cashing benefits, going on a bus, collecting a brother or sister from school, rocking the baby to stop it crying, chasing a cat or exercising a dog, even making a cup of tea.

The staff implicitly deny that the nursery is not a home, and try to convince themselves that it is; that they can substitute for the (idealized) mother–child experiences which the child is deemed to be lacking. This accounts for the overstaffing in some of the nurseries, and the belief that the child is incapable of learning anything valuable unless in a one-to-one situation. In one of the nurseries I have come across they had even invented a verb to describe the process – *one-to-oneing*. This seemed to involve sitting down next to a child – or summoning him or her to a table – and murmuring questions and instructions in his or her ear about whatever he or she was playing with; at one level a very oppressive technique to impose (since it rarely seemed to be self-chosen) on a vulnerable child trying to establish his or her autonomy.

This view of the job as substitute mothering was also borne out in a separate study commissioned by the DfEE (Penn and McQuail, 1997). We interviewed several cohorts of student nursery nurses. The majority of these nursery nurses when asked to define their role clearly saw themselves in some sense as substitute mothers; but their mothering was confined to mimicking the tones of motherhood in an instructional situation rather than being able to recreate the home itself.

Again it is not that the staff were lacking in their attempts to provide for the children. The point is there are few theoretical alternatives to the individualistic point of view, there is no bank of ideas or knowledge which staff could draw on to develop an alternative viewpoint, one which is much more positive about the collective opportunities which a nursery could provide and which offers practical propositions derived from what Malaguzzi calls 'a theory of relationships'.

Finally in this critique of developmental psychology as an underpinning knowledge base for work in nurseries, there is the trenchant, and increasingly frequently voiced criticism that it shuts out the irreducibly complex real world. This is put vividly by the historian Michael Zuckerman (1993, p. 231) who claims that social, cultural and historical insights and findings are routinely denied by developmental psychologists: 'Do developmentalists really want to know? Are they actually ready to deal with what they say they are? Can they truly abandon the positivist presumption of homogeneity and give up the positivist goal of universality? Can they authentically accept radical contingency and indeterminacy and come to terms with situation-specific particularity?'

The enduring nature of children's subculture, the games they play with one another, has been known for a long while (Opie and Opie, 1969) but there is now a new focus on childhood, prompted partly by historians – stimulated by Aries' (1979) famous work, *Centuries of Childhood*; partly by sociologists, who focus on children as a distinct social group in relationship with other groups (Mayall, 1996); and partly by anthropologists who have been charting the very different concepts of childhood held in different cultural groups (Levine *et al.*, 1994). These sociologists, anthropologists, historians – but rarely developmental psychologists – are increasingly studying childhood as a cultural phenomenon, and the variations in its interpretation, both historically and geographically – the child in time and space. This study of childhood includes examination of the ways in which children are treated by society, both informally, and formally in the sense of their recognition and acknowledgement in the formal institutions of the state – in the law, in the collection of national statistics and so on:

> Childhood is a social phenomenon. It is so in the sense that every society crystallizes its own set of norms, rules and regulations which dictate its attitudes towards the category of its members defined as children. This attitude towards children stems from the highest moral values of society that define the essence of a person. The most prominent characteristic of a *child* according to any definition, is that he/she is not (yet) an adult. Any other parameter of the definition of a *child* might change from one society to another, as well as within the same society, from one historical period to another, or from one social group to another. That is to say despite the strong biological determinants that are an integral part of this definition, the concept of the child is culture bound.
>
> (Shamgar-Handelman, 1994, p. 250).

Whilst this new emphasis on and status for childhood is very welcome, it accentuates diversity and inclusivity. Far from postulating the universal decontextualized child with his or her unvarying age-related sequences of development, the child is disclosed – often using his or her own voice – as an actor and commentator on events, deserving of recognition. Zelitzer (1985) in a much cited and elegant study, traces the development of the child from someone who is an economic contributor to the family, into someone who is economically valueless but emotionally priceless. Other studies show how children's views of what is happening differ substantially from those of the adults around them (Hood *et al.*, 1996).

In this broader context it makes little sense to be prescriptive about young children, to legislate for their cognitive or socio-emotional development, or even for that matter to insist on a standardized notion of equal opportunities – another contemporary cliché. To quote Zuckerman (1993, p. 240) again:

> We can hardly do the most elementary empirical work, let alone the more theoretical exercise if we do not address these questions of competing realities, or at least competing claims on reality. We cannot pronounce reliable regularities on which to base predictions because we cannot countermand the inexorable contingency of the human condition.

I have been arguing that there is not very much to go on in the UK by way of theory which can inform practice in nurseries, and that child development as an underpinning discipline is something of a dead end; whist offering rare insights into very particular situations, it can too easily lead to narrow and simplistic thinking rather than an opening out of possibilities and a recognition of Kessen's 'awesome variety of mankind'. But that does not make the enterprise of theorizing redundant, far from it. It makes it more necessary to describe, to think about and speculate about what we do and why, to explain this accumulation and accretion of practices which go on in nurseries, – many of them redundant or counterproductive – and to provide a rationale for changing them. In the rest of this chapter, I look at three examples of these practices – access, and health and safety, and hierarchy – which emerged from the study and consider why they have evolved, and what might be done to bring about changes.

Access to nursery

In the UK day nurseries there were a series of related practices about how and why children gained access to a day nursery place.

These practices emerged partly because of the gross shortage of places and the need to ration them to those most acutely 'in need' although as Audit Commission (1996) has pointed out, the definition of need varies considerably between local authorities in the UK sample. This rationing had led to elaborate procedures; all nurseries were issued with several pages of instruction notes on the stages in the admissions procedure, and what decisions had to be taken at what point and by whom.

A stilted, officious and badly printed version of these notes was also given to parents; they were told how their applications were going to be processed, and what redress they might have if they felt the procedure had not been fully implemented, but nowhere were they told what the nursery was for and what their child might hope to gain as a consequence of coming. This led to some tragi-comic misunderstandings. I sat in on one interview with a parent, a father whose wife had left him and who had come into the nursery to ask for a place. The father said over and over again that he was seeking a nursery place for his son because he felt his little boy was lonely and needed to get out of the house to play with other children; he was a bit of a handful and his grandmother who helped look after him felt that he would be better off where there was room to play about. The nursery officer-in-charge on the other hand did not comment at all on his stated reasons for seeking a place. Instead she concentrated on his status as a single father. She was determined to extract the story from him about when and why his wife had left him, a story which he clearly felt embarrassed about telling. She concluded the interview by recommending that he go to social services to seek marriage counselling, but was vague about whether his son could get a place at the nursery, and said she would refer the matter to the next admissions panel, although she could not say exactly when that would be. She handed him a copy of the leaflet to explain the referral procedure.

The procedures were intended to protect staff against potentially disruptive parents who might wish to question the rationing system. But this rationing was not a decision that could be made by the nursery; it had to be made elsewhere in the system, by a panel of social workers and health visitors, whose criteria were to do with family support, and the need to prevent family breakdown, rather than with any perceived need of the child. Servicing this panel, providing case notes, setting up meetings which everyone could attend, recording the decisions, reporting back on the 'progress' of the child to case conferences, answering queries about applications in the pipeline, all took a great deal of time. In addition in order to be 'fair' the places were shared out between several applicants, and slotted into whatever gaps were available. Hence a child might be given an afternoon here, two mornings there, and his or her irregular pattern of attendance would not match that of any other child. Moreover since the process was very slow, there were frequently vacancies held over whilst decisions were being made, although the nurseries had to be kept fully staffed, to their already generous ratios. Since only children from the most difficult family cases were admitted, the nurseries had a majority of children who were very distraught, and in some cases quite frenzied. This concentration of children with difficulties, with staff who were ill-prepared to deal with them and unsure about the personal or organizational strategies they might use to check some of the more destructive behaviour, led to very uncomfortable and tense atmospheres. It is a tribute to the patience and tolerance and persistence of some of the staff that the situation did not get more out of hand.

Given the process of admittance, that is only those parents whose problems were perceived as severe could have places for their children, the parents themselves were not considered as worthy or able enough to have any say as equals or colleagues in the running of the nurseries. There was a rhetoric about parental participation, but no parents participated in anything except an occasional fête, where the social situation and the roles were easier. Even then, parents were likely to be patronizingly praised, for example one mother who handled the takings at a jumble stall was introduced to me effusively by the officer-in-charge. 'Mary added all that by herself, how much have you made, Mary?' as if the mother was usually incapable or without integrity in handling money. Hence too the open-mouthed astonishment at the mother who had appeared in the television series discussing modern art.

Administering this patchwork system of attendance in the nursery consumed most of the time of the officer-in-charge, although much of this administration was routine paperwork, and could easily have done by a clerical assistant. Nor was there any technical assistance. Almost everything was written by longhand, and the attendance charts were card systems pinned to a wall. Unless the officer-in-charge tried very hard to make it otherwise, her primary job had less to do with the children and more to do with the rationing and allocation of places.

What had started off as an attempt to be fair had escalated into a set of inefficient self-protective bureaucratic procedures which ignored the effect on the children and parents, and swallowed the time of the officer-in-charge which might have been better spent as a skilled practitioner helping younger and more inexperienced staff deal with the more difficult children. There was no rationale about the needs of children to counterbalance and weigh against these time-consuming and self-justificatory procedures, and there was no opportunity or mechanism for staff within the nurseries for challenging them, or for parents to ask about the kind of care and education their children might receive. Abolishing this admissions panel procedure was one of the first steps taken in the UK local authority when changes were made.

Health and safety

Another obsessive set of practices concerned ideas about health and safety. Young children are naturally full of movement, like puppies or kittens, and given the opportunity they run, skip, hop, jump, tumble – they are frisky and the one way of moving which is unnatural to them is to walk sedately. Moreover parents generally encourage and celebrate young children's physical achievements – learning to walk, to hold a spoon, ride a bike, etc. Physical well-being and energy also depend on diet and rest. Children need to eat well and nutritiously, to enjoy eating; and to rest when they are tired. They need comfortable and predictable routines within which they are allowed a great deal of freedom.

In the UK day nurseries just the opposite happened. Children's physical existence was closely regulated and curtailed, and the routines, although predictable, did not recognize children's basic physical needs. The children were rarely allowed to move *except* sedately, because their rooms were so small and crowded and they were allowed outside so infrequently – in one case they were not allowed outside at all for 18 months! Eating was often a tense affair, rather than a celebratory one, and there was nowhere for tired children to rest. Rooms were poorly ventilated, and because of the proximity of toilets, sometimes smelly. Moreover the children were relentlessly exposed to adult gaze. There was nowhere in any of the nurseries for a child to hide or to play away from this constant surveillance.

Why were children treated in this way? Again it is partly that there was no theory about what children might want or need. Instead a set of practices had arisen which had the main function of reassuring staff that at all times children were safe and not likely to come to harm in their presence. This was important because some of the children had been abused, and staff saw it as a significant duty not only to identify such physical abuse, but to make absolutely sure that they were not seen to perpetuate it – so for example the child who wriggled and fell off a little chair when he was listening to a story was rushed to the office and the incident was entered in the accident book; or the clump of nettles in the garden which was regarded as a major hazard, so that children were no longer allowed to play in that corner until council workman had been to cut the nettles down (the nursery had to wait for weeks for someone to come and it simply did not occur to them to pull up the nettles themselves).

Outside play was regarded in three out of the four UK nurseries with nervousness, partly because of the number of very distraught children in the nurseries. Yet some of these children seemed desperate to have physical freedom. For instance the child who was totally uncommunicative within the room, and who restlessly barged from table to table apparently unaware of any other person, smiled and relaxed outside and was able to initiate a co-operative game with another child. But children were seen as being less under control outside, as evading surveillance and as more prone to accidents; so even when they were allowed to play outside, the play spaces for the most part were barren places, and the toys were dull. The weather was almost always regarded as unseasonable – rain was a deterrent but so was sunshine, because of the perceived problems of sunburn and skin cancer. Moreover the most popular training need which staff identified for themselves was first aid. Staff who had had no other in-service training had been on a first-aid course. If, in the unlikely event a child does have an accident, then they will know what to do.

The Children Act which regulates daycare provision has a substantial section on health and safety regulations, which have been zealously interpreted by those responsible for registration and inspection, because they are perceived as tangible and incontrovertible evidence of caring. If every conceivable risk is identified and removed, then parents can be assured of their children's safety, and the staff and the registration officers can be seen to have done their duty. But such anaesthetized unventilated surveyed spaces are dreary and constricting for the children themselves. They offer no opportunities for fun, games, co-operation, secrecy, exploration, movement, exertion or challenge or even fresh air. As Ward (1994, p. 182) has pointed out: 'The most teasing and tantalizing of these characteristics, that most of us would like to see in children, is that of resourcefulness in making use of their environment, simply because it involves those other attributes of responsibility and reciprocity.'

The day nurseries then were reinforcing a lack of resourcefulness in the children they cared for. Within nursery education, where, despite the emphasis on cognitive development, there is more of a coherent rationale and more of a tradition of outside play, these ferocious limitations are less in evidence, and in any case the health and safety regulations do not apply to the education sector. In the city where the research was carried out there were several excellent nursery schools which had large sloping grounds – with hidey holes, prickly shrubs, large trees with tyres and ropes hanging from them, climbing apparatus and a great variety of outside equipment and toys – to which children had free access for much of the day. These nursery schools had a nil accident rate, or perhaps the occasional cut or bruise was not considered particularly noteworthy; but no comparison was drawn between the freedom of the education regime and the virtual imprisonment of the day nursery regime. Paradoxically, in the day nurseries the preoccupation with health and safety had led to children being less healthy, and less able to deal with any kind of physical risk.

This issue began to be addressed by the new management of the day nurseries, and various consultants and specialists were brought in to help upgrade and change the way in which outside space was used. However, the more fundamental problem, more than the environment itself, was the engrained staff attitudes towards health and safety and the fear about the security of the children. Again there was no rationale, no coherent alternative on which to draw as an explanation for why practice should change.

Contradictions, hierarchy and training

With two exceptions all the staff in the UK nurseries were qualified, and those who were in charge of the nurseries mostly had an extra qualification, the DPQS, a post-qualifying diploma in nursery nursing. As explained in Chapter 3, the conventional training for those working in day nurseries is a qualification in nursery nursing, a diploma, a certificate or an equivalent national vocational qualification which is based on workplace assessment. These courses relied heavily on the assumptions about child development and mothering discussed above. This qualification can be obtained after two years' study or practice post-16 and has an academic equivalence of roughly one 'A' level. Neither the college-based qualifications nor the vocational qualifications are eligible for mandatory grants. Nor are they normally a sufficient qualification for university entrance. The training then is vocational and non-academic, and is not a career route to anywhere else. It is a relatively low-level specialist training.

This lack of status for training in nursery work is much lamented (Pugh, 1996), but because it is seen as an undemanding course, it attracts many students who have been deterred from a more academic route, and who have experienced educational failure. In the study described above of students in childcare training (Penn and McQuail, 1997), a majority of them expressed ambivalence about and hostility towards teaching and education. Instead they saw nursery nursing as building on skills and aptitudes that they already possessed. Many of them considered that motherhood and/or their experiences of caring for children made them 'naturals' for working with young children. The most frequently mentioned qualities that were seen as important in caring for children – patience, kindness, understanding, tolerance, flexibility, consistency, reliability – were seen as qualities that women brought with them rather than qualities they acquired through training. Many women turn to childcare as a profession because it is perceived as easy and unthreatening; it builds on what they already know and think they can do, and it does not carry too many risks. The essence of their activity is 'being with' the children, preferably on a one-to-one basis.

This basic training then was regarded as being sufficient evidence of competency. There was no culture of training in the nurseries, there were no books, no professional magazines, not even the popular and accessible magazine *Nursery World* which is aimed at nursery nurses. There was no discussion, formal or informal, which indicated that there were interesting or contentious issues to be discussed. Those few staff who had been on in-service courses had mostly attended one-day or half-day courses on topics like first aid, health and safety or child abuse. Staff kept their heads down and got on with their work.

Why was there such unreflective practice? Partly it was because the local authority had allowed no time for in-service training, and had considered it too costly and unnecessary. But it was also to do with the nature of initial training and those who were attracted to it as a vocational rather than as an academic course. It was to do with the nature of the courses which assumed that a basic introduction to child development was a sufficient knowledge base for the complex practices and organizational culture within the nurseries. The view that nursery nurses have of themselves as drawing on natural skills of 'mothering' is reinforced by the view, so powerful within social work, that the strength and quality of mother–child relationships are so important that only under exceptional circumstances should a child be removed and put in a day nursery; and then – as described above – only if the nursery tries to replicate the personal relationships of the home in relation to the things a child *ought* to be doing, that is playing with stimulating toys in order to advance his or her developmental progress.

A key worker system was in place, whereby one member of staff was supposed to relate closely to one identified child. This fiction of 'key workers' or substitute mothering was maintained although in practice it was impossible to operate because of the irregular attendance of the children and staff shifts. Moreover although these key worker relationships were supposed to be a source of comfort and reinforcement for the children, the staff rarely hugged, kissed or cuddled a child, and in one nursery staff were only allowed to touch a child with protective plastic gloves – for health and safety reasons!

Above all, there were very few opportunities in the nursery for group action or group discussion, and there was no sense that it was important. Staff meetings were scheduled, but they were infrequent, and the agendas were mainly administrative – i.e. a discussion of the latest batch of instructions sent down from a senior manager in social services. The staff shifts, which had to cover nominal rather than actual attendance, and the organization of the service, whereby it was open throughout the year even at holiday periods when attendance was very low, meant that it was very difficult to build in times when staff met together. Staff ate with children, and then had staggered lunch and tea breaks, so there were no communal mealtimes for informal chat or exchange of information. There were no shared pleasures as in the Italian and Spanish nurseries.

Just as the children were individuals ranked by their developmental status, so the staff were individuals ranked by their hierarchical status. The staff had to fit in with the requirements of the job as laid down for them by officer-in-charge, that is the hours they attended, and the rooms of children they serviced. Given the hierarchies within the nurseries, the more junior staff were timid about advancing their views. The main avenue for them to say what they were feeling was through their 'supervision sessions' with the very managers to whom they were expected to be deferential, and although staff were polite and loyal when talking to me, they were more critical when they could use the anonymity of the questionnaires. In one nursery for example, the staff felt resentful because they felt the officer-in-charge manipulated the shifts to her own advantage, and she and her deputy gave themselves more favourable times; whereas the officer-in-charge described herself as fair and open and committed to listening to her staff's grievances!

The opening of the nursery had at all times to be covered by the officer-in-charge or her deputy. The deputy who, like the officer-in-charge, was supernumerary had no real function other than that of stand-in. There was no job description. One deputy spent all her time during the study organizing a jumble sale and sale of work; another described her job as liaising with the buildings officer over health and safety. The main reason for the post was to make sure that a 'senior' person was there to be held responsible if anything went wrong whilst the officer-in-charge was away, since more low-status staff could not be allowed to assume such responsibilities for the running of the nursery.

There is an increasing amount of rhetoric about 'leadership' in the nursery (Rodd, 1994) but there is none about 'followership'. A leader cannot be a leader without followers, who are paid less and have less autonomy. Given these inherent and sometimes irreconcilable tensions of management, even in the best of circumstances things go wrong. What can followers do about it? The problematic nature of these unequal hierarchical relationships are articulated by trades unions, and there is some protection for subordinates enshrined within employment law, but otherwise hierarchy is usually seen entirely from the point of view of managers. The hierarchical nature of these nurseries was not only unquestioned but also reinforced at every turn, and the only protection the more junior or subordinate employees had against unjust decisions was through union action. Consequently the managers were very antagonistic to the union because it challenged their point of view. The woman who was the union shop steward for the nursery nurses was described to me in very derogatory and half-fearful tones as 'a trouble-maker', because she voiced a point of view about procedures which was not acceptable to those in charge.

Given all these circumstances, the tenets of their training, the contradictions they faced at every turn, the depressed environments in which they worked and the traumatized children who came to them, and the hierarchical and individualistic nature of the nursery, it is hardly surprising that there was no culture of training within the nurseries. The staff did indeed show the qualities they considered necessary for the job and most of those whom I observed were astonishingly and admirably patient, tolerant, flexible and consistent with some very difficult children. But it was too painful and too difficult to think, to learn any more, to try to make changes. It was not merely a question of introducing more training which covered a wider range of subjects – short-term initiatives were simply doomed to failure, as in the most vandalized and disorganized nursery, which had held more training sessions than any other nursery. It was a question of making profound changes to the system, of challenging a whole range of practices which were antithetical to children, of developing alternative ways of thinking about and doing the work, of being able to draw on richer veins of theory. It was, in short, a cultural change which was necessary.

Making changes

In this authority, to its credit, this cultural change is now being attempted, with all the insecurity and conflict that comes from trying to change practice, particularly when resources are tight. The day nurseries are being taken away from social services control, and seen as part of a coherent service for all young children and their families, not just as a segregated service for those who are distressed and distraught. Close links are being forged with the sympathetic local university education department to try to articulate practice and locate it in theory, and vice versa, to illuminate and revise theory through the lessons of practice. There is support and advice readily available within the under-5s service. There is an understanding that parents can contribute significant understandings to practice in general, as well as to their own children in particular, and formal and informal ways of generating this kind of discussion are being considered. There are still no more places, but existing places are being used more sensibly. Staff hierarchies are being re-examined although the unions wish to make sure there are no losers in any reorganization – which is something of an impossibility given the redundant nature of some of the graded posts. There are other inner-city projects which are in a small way addressing inner-city poverty and trying to create employment.

This local authority is not unique. There are an increasing number of local authorities who are trying, against the odds, to develop services which are more in touch with the needs of families and children, and to deconstruct practices which are inimical to the interests of children. But many more, the majority, continue as they are, unthinkingly reproducing the inequalities and dismalness of poverty, reinforced by legislation which distorts what needs to be done, and relying on staff whose training is prescriptive.

But change there must be. It is truly shocking that children are, with the best of intentions, so badly treated in public day nurseries. This book is in no way intended as an argument against day nurseries, which, as the comparative material shows, can be very pleasant, merry and thoughtful places. Nor is it intended as a personal criticism of the staff who work in them, most of whom are hard-working and dedicated and deserve more recognition for their efforts. Instead I am offering an analysis of an unworkable system and making a plea for a more rational, more considered, more joyful service for young children. Utopia? Or within our grasp?

References and further reading

Andreoli, S. and Cocever, E. (1988) *I Quaderni dell'Infanzia: Al confini del nido: servizi per la prima infanzia all'estero.* Bologna, IRPA.

Aries, P. (1979) *Centuries of Childhood.* Harmondsworth, Penguin.

Audit Commission (1996) *Under Fives Count. A Management Handbook on the Education of Children Under Five.* London, Audit Commission.

Balaguer, I., Mestres, I. and Penn, H. (1992) *Quality in Services to Young Children. European Commission Discussion Paper.* Brussels, CEC, Director-General for Employment, Industrial Relations and Social Affairs.

Ball, S. J. (1993) Self-doubt and soft data: social and technical trajectories in ethnographic fieldwork, in Hammersley (ed.), op. cit.

Bassi, R. and Neri, A. (1980) *La Scuola dell'Infanzia e l'educazione psicomotoria.* Bologna, Societa editrice il Mulino/IRPA.

Belle , D. (ed.) (1989) *Children's Social Networks and Social Supports.* New York, Wiley.

Bonomi, G. and Righi, O. (1982) *Una Stagione Pedagogica con Bruno Ciari.* Bologna, Societa Editrice il Mulino/IRPA.

Bowlby, J. (1951) *Maternal Care and Mental Health* Geneva: World Health Organization.

Brannen, J. and O'Brien, M. (1995) *Childhood and Parenthood. Proceedings of the International Sociological Association Committee for Family Research Conference, 1994.* London, Institute of Education.

Bronfenbrenner, U. (1979) *The Ecology of Human Development.* Cambridgbe, Mass., Harvard University Press.

Bronfenbrenner, U., Kessel, F., Kessen, W. and White, S. (1986) Towards a critical social history of developmental psychology, *American Psychologist*, Vol. 41, no. 11, pp. 1218–30.

Bull, J., Cameron, C., Candappa, M., Moss, P. and Owen, C. (1994) *Implementing the Children Act for Children Under 8.* London, HMSO.

Burgard, R. (1994) *The Frankfurt Nursery Programme.* Frankfurt, Archigrad.

Cahan, E., Mechling, J., Sutton-Smith, B. and White, S. (1993) The elusive historical child, in Elder *et al.* (eds.), op. cit.

Christopherson, S. (1997) *Caring as a Gendered Occupation.* Paris, OECD.

Ciari, B., in Lamb, M., Sternberg, K., Hwang, C., and Broberg, A. (1992) *Child Care in Context.* London: Lawrence Erlbaum.

Cocever, E. (ed.) (1990) *Bambini attivi e autonomi: A cosa serve l'adulto? L'esperienza di Loczy.* Firenze, La Nuova Italia.

Cochran, M. (1993) *International Handbook of Childcare Policies and Programmes.* Connecticut/London, Greenwood Press.

Cohen, L. and Manion, L. (1994) *Research Methods in Education.* London, Routledge.

Corsaro, W. (1985) *Friendship and Peer Culture in the Early Years.* Norwood, NJ, Ablex.

Corsaro, W. and Emiliani, F. (1992) Child care, early education, and children's peer culture in Italy, in Lamb *et al.* (eds.), op. cit.

Dahlberg, G (1995) Pedagogy and social context. Paper given at a Baring Foundation Seminar, Institute of Education, September.

Department of Health *The Children Act 1989 Guidance and Regulations, Vo.* 2. London, HMSO.

Department of Health (1996) *Children's Day Care Facilities at 31 March 1995. England.* Prepared by the Government Statistical Service.

DfEE (1996) *Work and Family: Ideas and Options for Childcare: A Consultation Paper.* London, Department for Education and Employment.

Dunn, J. (1993) *Young Children's Close Relationships. Beyond Attachment: Individual Differences and Development Series,* 4. London, Sage.

Elder, G., Modell, J. and Parke, R. (eds.) (1993) *Children in Time and Space: Developmental and Historical Insights.* Cambridge, Cambridge University Press.

Emiliani, F. and Zani, B. (1984) Behaviour and goals in adult–child interaction in the day nursery, in Doise, W. and Palmonari, A. (eds.) *Social Interaction and Individual Development.* Cambridge, Cambridge University Press.

European Commission Network on Childcare (1996) *A Review of Services for Young Children in the European Union 1990–1995.* Brussels, Equal Opportunities Unit DGV.

European Childcare Network (1966) *A Decade of Achievement.* Brussels, European Commission, DGV.

Frankenburg, S. (1934) *Common Sense in the Nursery.* London, Penguin Handbook (1945 edition).

Freire, P. (1996) *Letters to Christina: Reflections on my Life and Work.* London, Routledge.

Ghedini, P. (1987) *Asili nido tra esperienza e progretto.* Firenze, La Nuova Italia.

Goldschmied, E. and Jackson, S. (1994) *People Under Three.* London, Routledge.

Goody, J (1982) *Cooking, Cuisine and Class.* Cambridge, Cambridge University Press.

Grieve, R. and Hughes, M. (eds.) (1990) *Understanding Children.* Oxford, Blackwell.

Hammersley, M. (ed). (1993) *Educational Research*. London, Paul Chapman.

Hood, S., Kelley, P., Mayall, B. and Oakley, A. (1996) *Children, Parents and Risk*. London, Social Science Research Unit, Institute of Education, University of London.

Hutton, W. (1995) *The State We're In*. London: Jonathon Cape.

James, A. and Prout, A. (1990) *Constructing and Reconstructing Childhood*. Brighton, Falmer Press.

Jorde-Bloom, P. (1988) *Early Childhood Work Environment Rating Scale*. Urbana-Champaign, Ill., University of Illinois Press.

Kessen, W. (1983) The child and other cultural inventions, in Kessel, F. S. and Siegel, A. W. (eds.) *The Child and Other Cultural Inventions*. New York, Praeger.

Kessen, W. (1993) A developmentalist's reflections, in Elder *et al.* (eds.), op. cit.

Lamb, M., Sternberg K., Hwang, C. and Broberg, A. (1992) *Childcare in Context*. London, Lawrence Erlbaum Associates.

Langsted, O. (1994) Looking at quality from a child's perspective, in Moss, P. and Pence, A. (eds.) *Valuing Quality*. London, Paul Chapman.

Levine, R., Dixon, S., Levine, S., Richman, A., Leiderman, P. H., Keefer, C. and Brazelton, T. (1994) *Childcare and Culture. Lessons from Africa*. Cambridge, Cambridgbe University Press.

Levi-Strauss, C. (1968) *The Origin of Table Manners*. London, Jonathan Cape.

Lewis, C. (1995) *Educating Hearts and Minds*. Cambridge, Cambridge University Press.

Liddell, C. and Kemp, J. (1995) Providing services for young children in South Africa, *International Journal of Educational Development*, Vol. 15, no. 1, pp. 71–8.

Malaguzzi, L. (1993) For an Education Based on Relationships. NAEYC. *Young Children*, November. 1993., pp. 10–12.

Mata y Garriga, M. (1990) *El Futuro de la Educacion Infantil*. Madrid, Congreso Internacional de Educacion Infantil: Aspectos Juridicos y Sociales. Consejeria de Educacion.

Mayall, B. (ed.) (1994) *Children's Childhoods Observed and Experienced* London, Falmer.

Mayall, B. (1996) *Children, Health and the Social Order*. Buckingham, Open University Press.

Mead, M. (1963) *Growing up in New Guinea*. London, Penguin.

Ministerio de Educacion y Ciencia (1989) *Ejemplificaciones del Diseno Curricular Base: Infantil y Primeria*. Madrid, MEC.

Morss, J. (1990) *The Biologizing of Childhood*. Hillsdale, NJ, Lawrence Erlbaum Associates.

Moss, P. (1988) *Childcare and Equality of Opportunity. Consolidated Report to the European Commission*, V/746/88-EN. Brussels, European Commission.

Moss, P. and Penn, H. (1996) *Transforming Nursery Education*. London, Paul Chapman.

Mozere, L. (1992) *Le Printemps des Crèches: Histoire et analyse d'un mouvement*. Paris, Harmattan.

Olmsted, P. and Weikart, D. (eds.) *How Nations Serve Young Children*. Ypsilanti, Mich., High Scope Press.

Opie, I. and Opie, P. (1969) *Children's Games in Street and Playground*. Oxford, Oxford University Press.

Penn, H. (1994a) Private day nurseries in the UK. Report for BBC *Panorama*.

Penn, H. (1994b) Comparing concepts of learning in publicly funded day nurseries in Italy, Spain and Britain, *International Journal of Early Years Education*, Vol. 2, no. 3, pp. 54–67.

Penn, H. and McQuail, S. (1997) *Childcare as a Gendered Occupation*. London, (forthcoming).

Petrie, P. (1994) Quality in school-age child-care services: an inquiry about values, in Moss, P. and Pence, A. (eds.) *Valuing Quality*. London, Paul Chapman.

Phillips, D., Howes, C. and Whitebook, M. (1991) Childcare as an adult work environment, *Journal of Social Issues*, Vol. 47, no. 2, pp. 49–70.

Plowden Report (1967) *Children and Their Primary Schools. The Report of the Central Advisory Council for Education (England)*. London, HMSO.

Pugh, G. (ed.) (1996) *Education and Training for Work in the Early Years*. London: Early Years Training Group, National Children's Bureau.

Putnam, R. (1976) *The Comparative Study of Political Elites*. Englewood Cliffs, NJ, Prentice-Hall.

Qvortrup, J., Bardy, M., Sgritta, G. and Wintersberger, H. (1994) *Childhood Matters: Social Theory, Practice and Politics*. Aldershot, Avebury.

Reason, P. (ed.) (1994) *Participation in Human Enquiry* London, Sage.

Richman, N. and McGuire, J. (1988) Institutional characteristics of staff behaviour in day nurseries, *Children and Society*, Vol. 2, pp. 139–51.

Rodd, J (1994) *Leadership in Early Childhood Education. The Pathway to Professionalism*. Buckingham, Open University Press.

Salmon, P., Mortimore, P. *et al.* (1995) *School Effectiveness. Report for Ofsted*. London, Institute of Education.

Saraceno, C. (1977) *Experiencia y Teoria de las Comunas Infantiles*. Barcelona, Fontanella.

Serpell, R. (1993) *The Significance of Schooling: Life Journeys in an Afraican Society*. Cambridge, Cambridge University Press.

Shamgar-Handelman, L. (1994) To whom does childhood belong? in Qvortrup *et al.* (eds.) op. cit.

Stanton, A. (1989) *Invitation to Self-Management*. London, Dab Hand Press.

Tardos, A. (1984) Qu'est-ce que l'autonomie des le premier âge? *L'enfant*, Vol. 3–4, pp. 16–18.

Valiente, C. (1995) Children first: central government child care policies in post-authoritarian Spain, 1975–1994, in Brannen and O'Brien (eds.) op. cit.

Wachs, T. D. (1992) *The Nature of Nurture*. London, Sage.

Ward, C. (1994) Opportunities for childhoods in late twentieth century Britain, in Mayall, B. (ed.) op. cit.

Weinstein, C. and David, C. (1987) *Spaces for Children*. New York, Plenum Press.

Zelitzer, V. (1985) *Pricing the Priceless Child*, New York: Basic Books.

Zuckerman, M. (1993) History and developmental psychology, a dangerous liaison: a historian's perspective, in Elder, G. *et al.* (eds.) op. cit.

Index